THE SLOW PACE
OF FAST CHANGE

THE SLOW PACE OF FAST CHANGE

Bringing Innovations to Market in a Connected World

BHASKAR CHAKRAVORTI

Harvard Business School Press   *Boston, Massachusetts*

Library of Congress Cataloging-in-Publication Data

Chakravorti, Bhaskar.
   The slow pace of fast change : bringing innovations to market in
a connected world / by Bhaskar Chakravorti.
      p. cm.
      ISBN 1-57851-780-X (alk. paper)
      1. Technological innovations — Marketing. 2. Supply and demand.
   3. Rational choice theory. 4. Information theory in economics.
   I. Title.
      HC79.T4 C422 2003
      658.8 — dc21

                                        2002154818

To my parents

And my family, near and afar

CONTENTS

PREFACE

THE IDEAS IN THIS BOOK first saw the light of day in May 1998. I had written an opinion piece that appeared in London's *Financial Times* newspaper. The piece was apparently widely read, except that few could quite remember what it was about.

The popularity of my article could be traced to the *Financial Times* editors' inimitable British sense of fun; they had run the piece accompanied by a very attractive photograph of the actor Demi Moore.[1] It wasn't just the photograph that was at odds with the other items in the newspaper. The rest of the news was of *fast change*, with fresh examples from every corner of the globe. My article was a warning about its *slow pace*. The Dow closed at 8,937 and the NASDAQ at 1,781 on that day; both were destined to go higher. It is easy to see why so few of my readers could remember what the article actually had to say.

The ideas set forth in my article continued to develop with our work on the front lines of the many exciting innovations of the time attempting their forays into the marketplace. Often our advice and analysis suggested turning one way even when the headlines would make a march in the opposite direction more tempting. The experience in the field shaped the ideas, whereas the ideas shaped the experience. Naturally, the pace of my own writing was true to the title of the book; it progressed with deliberate speed. By the time I finished the manuscript in 2002, the newspapers had become much more accommodating to its thesis. In fact, the headlines had ventured well beyond that. With the fall of the likes of Enron and WorldCom, we learned of the lengths to which even the most innovative would go to obfuscate the true slowness of innovation's pace. With the fall of the twin towers of lower Manhattan, we realized the terrifying ramifications of a truly connected world.

These latter realities are by themselves complex topics and subjects for several other books. Nevertheless, they made me even more convinced of the importance of a framework for anticipating the effects on the pace of progress of the increasing entanglement of our decisions with decisions of others.

I have written this book with several audiences in mind. These include the executive who must take on the risk and investment in bringing innovations to market and lead an organization that relies on such innovations as a crucial competitive lever; the strategist and adviser who must frame the choices and guide action; and the academic and student interested in furthering our understanding of how connected markets work and how strategy and innovations transform them. More broadly, I hope to address a wider readership interested in progress and its pace in an interconnected world.

The style and contents of the book represent a synthesis of many perspectives. I have had the good fortune to draw on rather diverse experiences that have shaped my thinking on these issues.

I grew up influenced by historians, with a father of the oral kind and an uncle of the eminent kind. From them I have gained an appreciation for the past as a guide to what lies ahead—no matter how eager one is to leave that past in the dust, especially the kind of dust stirred up by exciting new technologies. Of course, the role of innovation is to make the future different from the past; therein lies the challenge. In the principles of game theory, a field I taught and did research on for many years, I found the structure I needed to build bridges between the past and the future. It yielded other benefits. As a game theorist, I found it second nature to anticipate the inevitable inefficiencies in markets—which automatically led me to treat unbridled expectations of fast change with some suspicion. This got me started on this line of inquiry in the first place.

My view of innovation and markets has also been shaped by many experiences. In my years on faculties in both university and high-tech R&D, I have witnessed and participated in the curious mixture of idealism, insularity, and creative energy that drives the very front end of the innovation process—and there is surprising commonality of these traits across both academia and industry. Monitor Group's extraordinary access to some of the most formidable players in the most innovative and challenging markets—particularly the telecommunications, high-technology, and health- and consumer-care markets— has given me an opportunity to participate at the opposite end as well: where innovation meets the market.

From my academic roots, I developed an appreciation for a first-principles approach to strategy and decisions. From my work at Monitor, I have learned how first principles translate into the framing of trade-offs and lead to timely action. From my clients in industry, I have learned to respect the courage and wisdom needed to be the ultimate bearer of risk—for risk is the other side of the coin of action. From my wife, Gita, I learned that true insight comes from connecting the dots across multiple landscapes. Through my children, Tarit and Sahana, I have found that such dots lurk in the unlikeliest of quarters. All these influences find their way in the contents that follow.

Much of the insight here was developed in the crucible of the real world. I have built on the work of many senior executives and colleagues at Monitor. I have also built on literature straddling many fields: strategy, innovation, game theory, marketing, and the economics of industrial organization. Instead of getting into individual citations and articles, I will briefly comment on the connections to some of the well-known books on these subjects, since they would be the most widely read. For this, I will borrow the words from a reviewer of this book:

> In my view, the relevant well-known authors with previous works adjacent to this space are Michael Porter, Barry Nalebuff, Adam Brandenburger, Pankaj Ghemawat, and Geoffrey Moore. This book fits into the existing literature in a very interesting way. While Porter (and many others) have focused on competition and competitive advantage in markets, Nalebuff and Brandenburger substantially added to that body of knowledge with their book *Co-opetition*. That started to introduce concepts of game theory and network effects into the strategy literature. However, the strategy literature has not been linked strongly to work on innovation, at least not for a general business audience. Geoffrey Moore's *Crossing the Chasm* set out a framework for thinking about launching an innovation into a market. . . . Chakravorti's book is a successor . . . taking it beyond simple market adoption and into the realm of network effects. Another literature linkage is to the *Profit Zone* work of Adrian Slywotsky. While those books focused on the business design of the firm, Chakravorti's book goes further to look at the design of the firm's positioning in a network.[2]

Placed in such distinguished company, I will not complain. I will, however, add a few other names on the reader's list of books to which my ideas are related: Thomas S. Kuhn's *The Structure of Scientific Revolutions*, Everett M. Rogers's *The Diffusion of Innovations*, and James M. Utterback's *Mastering the Dynamics of Innovation*, which laid much of the groundwork for the thinking on how innovations have impact; Carl Shapiro and Hal R. Varian's *Information Rules* for making the connections between information networks and strategic choice; John Seely Brown and Paul Duguid's *The Social Life of Information* and Malcolm Gladwell's *The Tipping Point* for relating the penetration of new ideas to the role of social networks; W. Brian Arthur's *Increasing Returns and Path Dependence in the Economy* and Clayton Christensen's *The Innovator's Dilemma* for preparing us for seemingly paradoxical aspects of the innovation process and its relation to the status quo both outside and inside the organization; Jean Tirole's *The Theory of Industrial Organization* and Drew Fudenberg and Jean Tirole's *Game Theory* for the microeconomic fundamentals underlying strategy.[3]

I would like to acknowledge my gratitude to all those without whose help this project would not have been accomplished. In addition to the many client executives whose confidentiality I must preserve, I am most grateful to Joe Fuller for his unstinting support and encouragement over the years and for raising the right questions that motivated my search for answers. George Norsig saw the relevance of these ideas in both expected and unexpected quarters and provided continued encouragement, mentoring, and thought partnership. I thank Alan Kantrow for his careful reading of the manuscript and his insightful commentary on both the big and the little things. Bob Lurie inspired my interest in actionable theory—as opposed to theoretical action. I had few examples to turn to; he showed me it could be done. Thanks to Phil Minasian and Paul Magill, who have been intellectual partners and have helped develop many of my ideas around strategy and technology, and to Guy Cogan and Steve Jennings for bringing many client issues to my attention from which the ideas of the book developed. Partha Bose, Tom Keiser, Sandra Pocharski, and Peter Schwartz have helped push my thinking further in several conversations. Thanks to Tom Craig for helping raise awareness of this work, to Clayton Christensen for pointing out the linkages with his work, and to Julio Benedicto, Leigh Bivings, Rob Cheng, Katrin Kalischer-Stork, Ben Harley, and David Sandrich for taking the lead in applying these ideas in numerous client settings. I also extend my gratitude to Katrin Herrling, Eliette Krakora, Daniel Ramirez, and several other talented colleagues with whom I have had the privilege of working in numerous client engagements and benefiting from their insights, and to Nancy Nichols and Jeron Paul for comments on early thought pieces. I thank Dilip Abreu, Hal Cole, Satyajit Chatterjee, John Conley, Laurence Kranich, Arunava Sen, Mike Spagat, Yossi Spiegel, Ellis Tallman, Bart Taub, and Simon Wilkie, who have helped shape my ideas over the years.

I thank my wife, Gita, for being who she is—a partner in life and thought—and the two most wonderful children anyone can dream of, Tarit and Sahana, and my family spread out over two countries, the Chakravortis, the Kilaras, the Ramchandanis, and the Raos, for their constant encouragement and love. I would be remiss if I did not especially acknowledge my late father, Birendra Nath Chakravorti, for instilling in me the joy of writing as a child and William Thomson for instilling it again as a grown-up. My gratitude also goes to the many friends (whose names would fill the page—the only reason they do not appear individually) who cheered for the project's completion and kept me going with the ever inspirational "You mean you aren't done yet?" and with whom I have traded ideas in years past.

I have had the pleasure to work with Melinda Adams Merino, my editor at Harvard Business School Press, who helped visualize the book, provided thoughtful guidance and, amazingly, combined the gentle with the firm editorial touch. I am also deeply grateful to Bob Metcalfe, Barry Nalebuff, Sylvia Weedman, and six anonymous reviewers for commentary on earlier drafts and to the editorial team at Harvard Business School Press, especially Jill Connor and Astrid Sandoval, for their support during the final stages. Finally, thanks to Lizette Figueiredo, Judy Freeman, and Cynthia Mastroianni for their bright smiles and warmth every day at Monitor.

Alas, I stand alone in bearing responsibility for all errors.

In the meantime, the subject of my book, the connected world, continues to turn and raise new questions, tempting yet another chapter to be added. The futurist Peter Schwartz had warned me that you never finish a book; you only have it taken away from you. In that spirit, dear reader, it is now your turn to take it away.

Bhaskar Chakravorti
Cambridge, Massachusetts
October 2002

THE SLOW PACE

OF FAST CHANGE

Chapter One

A BEAUTIFUL BIND

For it is a secret, both in nature and state,
that it is safer to change many things than one.

—Francis Bacon, *Essays, Civil and Moral,* vol. III

INNOVATIONS AND MARKETS have always made for an awkward match. The journey from invention in the lab to impact in the living room can be a maddeningly slow one, even for the most pathbreaking of ideas. It is also a journey that can take many unexpected and unplanned turns.

For one, many good ideas now canonized as revolutions took decades to have impact. We are often reminded by those mindful of history that canals, railways, and electrification did not appear overnight. Consider television, that most ubiquitous of innovations, which took more than thirty years—from GE's first TV program in 1928 to the 1960s—before becoming a true mass medium. Past history is, however, not the most reliable predictor of history yet to be made. TV's precursor, radio, had spread remarkably quickly at a pace "much more amazing than any other thing we have seen in our time," according to Herbert Hoover, then secretary of commerce.[1] Despite the

1

slow pace of innovation's progress in the market, some innovations do become hits and, frequently, in unexpected ways.

On the other hand, some innovations appear, only to disappear without a trace. Even here there can be surprises: They can reappear at a different time — sometimes a century or more later. Internet-savvy music aficionados are aware of the efforts of RealNetworks, Microsoft, and the five major music labels to create Web sites that distribute music on demand over the network for a price. Their efforts were meant to bring these same aficionados back from the clutches of disruptive upstarts with names like Napster, Grokster, and Madster. The pay-as-you-listen, music-on-demand idea had been tried before. The Tel-musici Company had set up such a service based out of Wilmington, Delaware, over the telephone network. The price: three cents for "ordinary" music and a hefty seven cents for grand opera. The time: 1909.[2] Plans to set up music sites across the entire United States apparently never materialized.

The question of innovation's travels — and travails — in the market has new immediacy, given the revolutionary changes anticipated with the arrival of the information age and, of course, its accompanying miscalculations. There was good reason to anticipate that the innovation-market encounter would finally become less awkward. Information technologies were aiming to transform both innovation *and* the market, potentially making their match a little more compatible. Advances in computing, communications, and networking technology were expected to stimulate innovations across all industries. Simultaneously, these very advances would give life to a fabled curiosity from old economics textbooks: a perfect market. Here, information would flow freely, prices would adjust instantly to ups and downs in demand and supply, and the costs of transaction and search would simply melt away.

In principle, the benefits of innovation would carry over effortlessly into this friction-free, highly interconnected networked market. Inefficiencies would be matched to solutions quickly, and the solutions would be disseminated efficiently. The wider the network, the greater the value created for those who were part of it.[3] Innovation would finally deliver on the expectations of fast change on the back of such self-reinforcing network effects.

Entire firms were built with this premise in mind: Healtheon/WebMD, WorldCom, boo.com — the list is extraordinarily long. Other firms completely reinvented themselves. Enron jettisoned assets prized in the industrial age — oil rigs, pipelines, and power plants — in favor of broadband content-delivery networks and high-tech trading floors. Each, in different ways, discovered that, much like canals, railways, and electricity, the more recent revolutions must also contend with the slow pace of fast change, that is, the pace at which innovation enters and disperses through the market.[4]

Should we find this surprising? Perhaps. There was, after all, the confident promise of the network effect. There was the steady drumbeat of media-driven expectations about the advancing frontiers of technology. Although earlier economic systems — the markets, say, into which TV or Tel-musici had launched — have always been networked to some degree, the intensity and spread of information technology had made people expect that *this* time, things would really be different.

We were, after all, on the information superhighway. By all accounts, the vehicle of technology was accelerating. Trapped in the backseat, we are left asking, Are we there yet? The innovator may well ask, How do I get behind the steering wheel, and what should I look for with no posted signs on the road?

This book addresses these questions and offers some potential ways to recognize the slow pace of fast change, find its causes, and develop strategies to use this pace for market advantage. This is a book about innovation — not about the management of innovation within the company, but what happens when it leaves the company's front doors. In particular, the focus is on how the innovator can succeed in an increasingly interconnected marketplace in which the participants' decisions are mutually entangled.

I first make the case that the slowness of innovation's progress is *because* of the intense connectedness, not *despite* it. The book exposes a different, perhaps unexpected, face of the network effect. This face may surprise many readers, particularly given the praise that the network effect has enjoyed in recent years. I then turn to the question of what to do about this state of affairs and present the more practical implications for readers interested in developing a strategy for bringing innovations into such markets.

The intellectual origins of the approach taken here—both the interpretive and the prescriptive parts of it—are distinctive. I use the science of choice in interconnected settings, game theory, to equip the reader to steer an innovation through this connected world. In the process, I hope to uncover a powerful application for a set of ideas that has thus far been among the least widely known—and yet the most fundamental—contributions of the theory.

I begin with the basic mind-set fundamental to bringing innovations to market in a connected world. Getting an innovation to market involves two thresholds that the innovation must cross on its path to impact. The first occurs at the status quo, the situation that the innovation is attempting to improve; the second is at the new outcome that the innovation seeks to create, where a significant portion of its adopters are made better off. These thresholds share a characteristic that fundamentally captures the way choices are made in an interconnected environment. This is the notion of *equilibrium*. I will briefly introduce this notion here and then develop its applications in subsequent chapters.

EQUILIBRIUM

John Forbes Nash's "beautiful mind" has become widely known with the best-selling book and movie on the subject.[5]

Those familiar with the story know of the Princeton mathematician who, after a lifetime of struggle with schizophrenia, won the Nobel Prize in economics for a mysterious discovery. His discovery has been described as being "as 'fundamental and pervasive' to the social sciences as is the discovery of the double helix structure of DNA to the biological sciences, because it unlocks the hidden structure of social interaction."[6]

The framework that I offer for recognizing the factors that govern the progress of innovations is an application of Nash's Nobel-Prize-winning discovery: equilibrium. It is the dynamic created when each critical player in an innovation's path— firm or consumer—acts in self-interest while expecting that others on the path will do the same. Nash's concept alerts us to the intuitive but often overlooked notion that one's strategic choice depends on the choices of others. As this network of critical-path players widens, the payoff to one's own choice depends even more on those of others. This fundamental interdependency governs what is adopted, and when, in a connected market. Given its centrality to strategies for bringing innovation to such markets, Nash's mysterious idea is pivotal—"fundamental and pervasive"—in determining the winners and losers in the game of innovation. Innovators can no longer rely on their own outstanding assets such as breakthrough technology or the ability to meet customer needs alone; the final payoff is locked into an entire network of choices made by other market participants following their own interests and concerns.

An understanding of the causes of a particular equilibrium and what would take it apart is key to an innovation's success. It sets good innovation-to-market strategy apart from the rest. For this reason, I call this notion "a beautiful bind."

The structural sources of the bind lie, of course, in the networked nature of the market. By network I mean more than what would qualify as such in a technical sense—as, say, a Cisco engineer might describe it. Some markets develop around physical networks; these include the canals, railroads, and electricity networks of earlier eras, but also include more contemporary communications, media, transportation, telephone, and computer networks.[7] These networks have physical links that connect members to each other and make them interdependent.

A networked market, however, could also mean a market in which the links are not physical. The interdependency between members of such a networked market may be for strategic, economic, or informational reasons. The members include firms, consumers, and other parties involved in the decisions that precede an innovation's adoption and productive use. I frequently refer to them collectively as the players on an innovation's critical path.

In Nash's framework, an equilibrium of choices occurs when each party in a market makes a choice that it considers to be the best one relative to available alternatives, assuming that all other parties in the network are doing the same. This is not very different from the thinking that shapes the adoption of new products in a connected market. Adoption choices by one market participant depend on the adoption choices of others. Because of such a product's newness, each participant is making some guesses—and wants to learn more—about what the others are doing or intend to do.

For example, think about making a choice in the context of really fun games, not the ones that model business problems or win Nobel Prizes. Consider the new generation of video-game consoles that involve innovation in multimedia applications and electronics. A target consumer, say, an eleven-year-old, is presented with three tempting choices: Sony's PlayStation2, Microsoft's Xbox, and Nintendo's Game-Cube. In addition to these choices, there may be others from different points in time: an old game console—say, the far more humble Sony PlayStation—or forthcoming generations of these products, which, almost surely, will push the envelope even further in their interactive graphics and networking capabilities.

Consider a hypothetical, but not entirely atypical, conversation that might accompany the choice.[8]

"Maybe we should go for the Xbox. These game consoles are becoming like regular computers. With so much of plain, old computing centered on Microsoft Windows, Xbox may give us more options for games and other applications down the road. If everyone else believes that Microsoft's products will be everywhere in the near future, Xbox will most likely be the better buy. Xbox will also rule in the longer term, since everyone will follow a similar logic and buy it. And then it makes sense that the widest variety of gaming software will also be written for Xbox, further confirming that it would be the better buy."

"But wait. Sony and Nintendo have been in the video-game business for a longer time. They are better at it and will keep video games from getting sucked into becoming just another PC clone. Both companies—especially Sony—have a head start. So there may be more game options for their consoles, and going with one of them, like Sony, may give us many more games. This would be especially true if everybody else is reasoning the same way, since there will be more games written for *this* system."

"Before we decide, I must find out what my friends are going to buy, because I want to trade games with them. They will want to know what I am buying as well."

"Sounds like they may have the same chicken-and-egg dilemma. They will want to know what we are buying before they commit to one of the three."

"Wait. It says here that one of the game console players has dropped its price to under two hundred dollars. If we wait it out, the others will drop their prices as well."

"And we have hardly used the old PlayStation. We have all these games that work with it. Maybe we should wait until Sony comes out with a PlayStation3, or make a decision to switch to Microsoft altogether once these devices are all better interconnected. Who knows? Maybe someday it will not matter who makes the console; they will be made by the Chinese and the competition is going to be over the different games that can be played in any console."

Although Sony certainly enjoyed a swift takeoff of its game console by launching it ahead of the competition, considerations such as those in the hypothetical conversation may act as a brake on uptake of game consoles overall in a more competitive field.[9] Note that the complexity of the choice comes not only because of the interconnectedness of one's beliefs about the competing offers, but also because of all the supporting products, such as games and other applications, that depend on these offers.

These considerations are examples of equilibrium behavior: One's choice is predicated on assumptions about the choices of others, and the choices of others are tied to similar assumptions. Further, in a highly innovative environment, the range of possible choices will change over time. As a result, the linkage between the choices exists not only *at* a point in time; it is also present *across* time. Each generation of video-game consoles competes with both future and past generations.[10]

Nash's idea, therefore, becomes our starting point for understanding the link between interconnected markets and the progress of innovation.

THE MIND-SET:
INTERPRETING THE PACE OF PROGRESS

Equilibrium is a point of pause—a dynamic pause, and not an empty space where the forces of change have been put to sleep. It represents a balance among the choices being made by the network of players essential for an innovation's adoption. To succeed, an innovation must achieve two things. It must induce multiple behaviors to unlock in a *coordinated* manner. And it must recoordinate outcomes in a new equilibrium.

To arrive at this result, the innovation must typically pass a *critical mass* of adopters. A critical mass is the point at which enough participants—firms and consumers—have chosen the innovation so that even more participants will make the same choice, but with substantially less active reinforcement from the innovator.[11]

There are several aspects of this idea to keep in mind. First, a highly interconnected market will have a tendency to seek equilibrium. Such a market is a collection of individual, inter-dependent participants with no formal means of coordinating expectations about what each other is doing. Equilibrium is the unwritten protocol—a set of expectations about the behav-iors of others on which each individual in this system bases his or her unilateral choices. In the video-game example, one such expectation was an eleven-year-old's speculation about what system his friends are likely to buy. Another expectation is his parents' conjectures of whether Sony, Microsoft, and Nin-tendo are about to engage in a price war, thereby making the investment in yet another expensive distraction from school or the playground a little more bearable. And then there are, of course, the expectations behind the scenes: among the busi-ness planning teams at Sony, Microsoft, and Nintendo and among the players that develop supporting applications.

Second, we can expect such an equilibrium to be tempo-rary; a major contributing factor for the transient nature of equilibrium is the potential for ongoing innovation. Even as eleven-year-olds around the globe settle on their choices for the current generation of game consoles, they and everyone else in the industry fully expect that a new round of next-generation games is already in development. In our framing of the problem, innovation is a *dis*equilibriating force.

This way of thinking helps us view the barriers to the adop-tion of an innovation and their underlying dynamics in a new light. The principal barriers can be found by uncovering the factors behind the equilibrium in the status quo *and* in the fu-ture outcome targeted by the innovation. It is hard to dismantle the status-quo equilibrium, which is why the past endures. It is also hard to synchronize the changes necessary to put in place a new equilibrium, so that the innovation can hope to endure as well. In this sense, there is resistance to innovation's adoption at both ends — when it enters the market and when it must firmly establish itself therein.

The result: change does take place, albeit slowly. When change happens quickly, many choices around the network have been induced — either by design or by the independent and simultaneous efforts of numerous players in the interconnected system. The innovator that wants to increase the chances of payoff or accelerate its arrival must, therefore, adopt a systemic perspective on the choices that must be influenced and then visualize a *coordinated* attack on the problem.

To be sure, innovation takes place in complex circumstances; many factors ultimately govern its success. The object of innovation — the product or process or new technology — must work and have demonstrable benefit. Technology, execution, management, and organizational issues must work as well. The robustness of the basic business proposition surrounding an innovation's introduction to the marketplace is also critical. So, too, is thinking about equilibrium. However, because of its relatively less tangible and potentially complex nature, it is an easy consideration to miss. And when missed, there are huge risks to the innovator and to the market that could benefit from the innovation.

Consider two additional examples. The first illustrates the barriers to change caused by the bind of a networked market. The second illustrates a healthy rate of change.

Health Care Unwired

The science of health care clearly involves the mastery of complex anatomical networks: the blood circulatory system, the central nervous system, the digestive system, and so on. The business of providing modern, efficient health care requires the mastery of different networks, which reside outside the human anatomy. Health-care delivery is a highly information-intensive business and involves communication of complex information in many different directions.

Consider a scenario of the system at work. A routine sick visit involves information exchange between patient and physician on many fronts: the patient's symptoms, insurance information, patient history, drug allergies, to name a few. This exchange may be followed by diagnosis, treatment, and the filling of a prescription in a pharmacy. In each of these situations, there is an exchange of information among an additional set of parties: the physician's office, labs, other clinical departments, consulting physicians, medical information sources, insurance companies, the pharmacist, and so on.

Despite all the information that must be exchanged, today's health-care system is quite poorly served by information technology. Physicians, their offices, and hospitals have traditionally been late adopters of even the most rudimentary forms of information technology. Currently, much of the data is stored and imperfectly shared over different systems, part electronic and part paper. A look at the banks of paper files behind the receptionist's desk on your next visit to a physician's office would confirm this. The effective cost of the inefficiencies of this information gap is an estimated $250 billion a year.[12]

This gap persists, even though other information-intensive sectors, such as financial services, adopted information technology early on.[13] Compounding the paradox are the tight relationship between health care and the scientific community, and the high educational levels of practitioners. In other settings, both factors are generally good predictors of the early adoption of innovative technology.

Technically, the solutions for closing the gap are available. Companies focused on information technology customized for health care have emerged and are implementing electronic patient records. Moreover, the Internet provides a way for physicians and others in the relevant networks to connect over a common medium without incurring the heavy up-front investments necessary to establish or deploy information technology systems from scratch. The health-care system as a whole could clearly benefit from these and other innovative solutions. Even without explicit quantification of the inefficiency, virtually everyone who experiences the health-care system can feel its sting. Why, then, the slow pace of wiring health care?

One reason may well be that the choices relating to the adoption of new technology are dispersed among the broad network of players who would be affected, several of whom are named in the scenario just discussed. The current choices may not be ideal, but they are in equilibrium. Each player knows what to expect of others. A pharmacist who cannot read a physician's handwriting on a crumpled prescription may find it aggravating but routine to call the office and reconfirm. The physician's office is aggravated but not surprised by the call. Each player's decision is reinforced by the decisions of others; each individual decision is motivated and informed by its own private and narrow context. As a result, no significant player has the incentive to unilaterally switch to a different set of choices that are more information-technology friendly, since no player credibly expects that the others will change as well.

Physicians, for example, have the incentive to switch over only if the other participants in the system also switch. After all, electronic connectivity requires the parties at both ends to use compatible systems. From any single physician's viewpoint, everybody else deals in paper or phone calls and in some limited, nonstandardized form of electronic media. Insurance companies have no reason to switch unilaterally unless all the physicians they deal with do as well. The same goes for pharmacies and labs. With the majority of physicians working in small, independent practices, no single physician is motivated to change unilaterally. Put these separate pieces together, and the health-care system is caught in a "bad" equilibrium.

The irony, of course, is that if an innovator could wave a magic wand and break the status quo by simultaneously changing the behaviors of all these parties, there is a "good" equilibrium at the other end. If most of them were to switch over in their beliefs to a new, connected paradigm, each player would be unilaterally motivated to actually switch. What each player *expects* of the others is important, since the choice of one must coordinate with the choices of the rest. This is an essential fact of life in an interconnected world.

Claudine Singer, a Jupiter Research analyst, remarked on the resiliency of the health-care status quo despite the obvious benefits of change: "When you talk about it in theory, it [change] makes complete sense, but health care is not a reasonable industry."[14] On the contrary, viewed through the lens of equilibrium, health care is *extremely* reasonable. No one switches behavior unless it is compatible with self-interest, given the completely reasonable expectation of self-interested behavior among others.

Barriers exist both at the front end (destruction of the status quo) and at the back end (creation of a new equilibrium) of an innovation's journey to market. "Perennial gales of creative destruction" was economist Joseph Schumpeter's celebrated description of the innovation process.[15] Taking down these barriers is my interpretation of his evocative idea.

There are, on the other hand, innovations that move to market surprisingly fast. This happens only when several initiatives exert pressure simultaneously at different points in the system in a reinforcing way. These pressures could be strategically coordinated by a single innovator or could arise from the confluence of independent actions by multiple motivated players. In the latter case, the actions are mutually supportive even without explicit coordination.

Bringing Digital Imaging into Focus

Kodak is the undisputed pioneer of popular photography. Its role in steering this innovation to popularity, however, goes well beyond the invention of easy-to-use cameras. By the close of the nineteenth century, the company had also mastered the art of coordinating the network needed for adoption. The Kodak roll-film camera, first launched in 1888, began the initial phase of the coordination with the famous line "Press the button, we do the rest." With this slogan, the company kept the network necessary for developing pictures quite small. This network was essentially limited to early enthusiastic consumers and the Eastman Dry Plate and Film Company, to which consumers would mail in cameras so that the company could develop and replenish the film.

The network widened with a lesser-known Kodak innovation of 1891: cameras that permitted daylight loading. Now users could load their own film and even remove it without having to send it back to Kodak's darkrooms every time the film ran out. This change expanded the network to film retailers, who were eager to stock Kodak supplies, and opened for the company the potential of recurring revenue streams. The wide availability of film and the growing network of adopters meant that photography would catch on. Then came the $1 Kodak Brownie camera in 1900. The inexpensive, easy-to-use camera spawned generations of amateur photographers. Each. convert recruited others, thereby creating an ever-wider network of adopters.[16]

Today, another round of fast change has been under way in the world of photography. This time, it involves the switch from roll film to a digital means of capturing and sharing pictures. Sales of digital cameras are growing rapidly. As in the case of other digital consumer appliances, prices have been falling, and the capabilities of digital cameras have been improving swiftly. Again, Kodak is participating in the change.

At this point, however, the similarity with Kodak's earlier revolution ends.

Kodak's reach across the adoption network is no longer what it was more than a century ago. In the status quo, in addition to Kodak and other makers of emulsion film, the network includes camera makers, retailers that sell rolls of film, firms that develop them, and consumers. The consumers' current behaviors include storing photographs in shoe boxes and albums, mailing them to friends and relatives, and, of late, scanning them for viewing over the Internet. Although the status quo is quite inefficient in its use of time and other resources, it is a familiar reality—one that people have been comfortable with for a long time. Comfort and familiarity, ordinarily, create a powerful glue and lend stability to an existing equilibrium.

The network of the future does away with the buying and developing of film. Instead, the network comprises digital camera makers; printer manufacturers; image-editing, developing, organizing, and storage software developers; online developing services; as well as computer and cell-phone makers and broadband communications players.

Despite the raw appeal of digital photography for the consumer, the complete experience depends on a network of players. How is this rather wide network recoordinating toward a new equilibrium? In contrast to the case of health care, in this situation there are many players, each with a limited amount of leverage, that share a common motivation: to establish a new digital equilibrium. As a result, with the many initiatives of resourceful players, a new equilibrium is coming together, even though there is no single dominant coordinator.

Consider the multitude of motivated players steering toward a common purpose: Kodak not only is interested in defending its core business threatened by the ongoing transformation, but is also looking for new avenues for growth. Hewlett-Packard's printing capabilities make the firm deeply

interested in wresting Kodak's historically predominant position. Software companies, PC makers, and even cell-phone
makers can foresee digital imaging as one of the high-potential
consumer applications that could help reposition PCs and
cell phones as devices to capture and manage images. Camera
manufacturers, such as Sony and Olympus, hope to ensure
that their business does not get taken over by the likes of
Kodak or Hewlett-Packard. Other players, such as the online
photo service Shutterfly, are a part of the digital photography
network. Each is motivated by its own interests but is taking
actions that one way or the other help to enable an *implicit*
coordination that nudges the network toward a mutually reinforcing, digital future.[17]

In sum, the take-up of digital photography is due more to
the simultaneous actions of several highly motivated players
than to Kodak's repeating its previous history of single-
handed pioneering. Such simultaneity in initiative is missing
in health care. Together, these examples convey an important
lesson: In a connected world, change through innovation requires a systemic switching of behaviors.

Taking a strategic perspective on the matter, one cannot always rely on the system to make the right moves in parallel;
the innovator must actively plan for *orchestrating* such an effort. The next section describes the tools required for crafting
such an orchestration strategy.

THE TOOL SET: A FRAMEWORK FOR
LAUNCHING A COORDINATED ATTACK

The network's tangle can hinder an innovation's journey
through the market, but its very interconnectedness can help
the journey as well. Consequently, the nature and timing of an
innovation's market impact may be quite counterintuitive to
those who organize a market linearly by its several components: consumer, competitor, supplier, and so on. As suggested

earlier, this book draws on techniques developed in the science of choice in interconnected environments — the discipline of game theory — that gained its most fundamental solution in Nash's beautiful bind.[18]

Game theory is, in essence, a general framework for reducing any strategic situation into the circumstances of individual players whose interconnected actions, together with external events, determine the outcome of the situation. It offers the players a unique perspective through a combination of circumstances and other conditions: (1) the players' understanding of their own options and those of others; (2) the unchangeable rules of play of the market; (3) what information and assumptions the players have; and (4) what the players believe their payoffs will be when they make certain choices and when other players make different choices.

By looking at these aspects, a solution in game theory can help predict both how the players might independently make decisions despite the linkages in their decisions and how each player would expect the others to behave. As such, the theory has found application in interpretation as well as prescription in a variety of settings.[19]

In the context of an interconnected market, the framework of game theory provides insights at several levels. First, in a connected environment, the publicly observable outcome that emerges from many parallel choices might be counterintuitive when viewed in the aggregate. We can, however, find an explanation for the outcome by reducing it to the private choices of individuals; this is, after all, the level at which decisions are made in a free-market setting. Each private action is generally much more intuitive, especially when its logic is considered within the confines of the narrower, private context. This context helps explain the somewhat puzzling resistance to new technology in the health-care system.

Next, the framework offers guidance on how to act on such interpretations and how to affect market behaviors. Reducing an overall market situation to the individual level helps us see the situation from the perspective of others and uncover ways to strategically intervene and influence their choices. It does so by revealing the linkages between the choices and, therefore, the linkages to each strategist's interventions. We can then anticipate where in the interconnected market strategic interventions will be most effective in orchestrating the behaviors of other market players.

Finally, the words *game* and *theory* themselves have taken on distinctive meaning in a market for innovation. In recent times, the events surrounding innovation, particularly those developed within the context of the new economy, *have* taken on the look and feel of a game. For example, a global auction for Elvis's dental records worth a few hundred dollars was running side by side with competitive bids and counterbids on global telecommunications companies worth hundreds of *billions* of dollars. As a universal scoreboard, the stock market was awarding eBay, the facilitator of the Elvis transaction, over 4 years, a market cap that took the venerable J. P. Morgan 150 years of transactions to achieve. The same scoreboard also erased more than $2 trillion of value from the telecommunications industry in a few months after the bids were won and the deals concluded. One trusts that Elvis's records have enjoyed greater longevity.

Nevertheless, the game feature of importance here is more fundamental. Interconnected markets, when viewed as the aggregation of choices of self-interested players, are identical to games in their structure. In a real game, we naturally speculate on the moves of the rest of the players before making our own move. In fact, the moves of others become the primary drivers of our strategy. This encourages us to look at the situation from the perspectives of others. Good game players excel at this form of reasoning. Technologists and innovators do not naturally begin with such an outside-in perspective, particularly one that builds on finding out what the field of other players intend to do. For this reason alone, the presence of the term "game" in the framing of the problem is a most helpful reminder of the fundamental challenge at hand.

Several aspects of the term "theory" are also worth noting. First, an approach grounded in a theory suggests a return to first principles of market behavior. This makes our perspective on innovation distinct from best-practices research or from efforts to analogize from success stories. I prefer first principles because they endure and survive the cycles that turn success stories into cautionary tales. Theory also means there is hard work to be done. It presents options and criteria that a strategist must consider and test before making the key choices; it does not offer instant recipes.

Second, a fair question would be to ask how the protagonists in the examples that follow stumbled on the theory's principles. Was an expert game theorist whispering in their ears? Most probably not. The principles and the resulting framework discussed here are based on the empirical reality of observing the choice processes of hundreds of firms and other market participants in multiple industries. Moreover, the actual behavior of these players is consistent with the predictions of the framework once the players have had an opportunity to learn and experience a situation — or similar structural aspects of the situation — a few times. Experienced managers behave *as if* they were expert practitioners of the theory within their familiar industry contexts.

Such observations are consistent with evolutionary interpretations of social behavior. With repeated experience, we are all programmed to become experienced managers and develop such "as if" expertise. Think of your own strategic wisdom in the most mundane, yet complex, tasks: finding the best route home from work through familiar traffic patterns during rush hour, playing a favorite game or sport, repeated negotiations on familiar issues, and so forth. (My seven-year-old beats every visitor to the house in Connect Four, a game with, in theory, 10^{13} positions to consider.) In each of these situations, you are probably making decisions as an expert theorist would. Like M. Jourdain in Molière's *Le bourgeois gentilhomme*, who was stunned to learn that he had been speaking prose all his life and hadn't known it, this latent expertise as a practicing game theorist may come as a complete surprise.

The trouble with the innovation-market encounter is that it generally creates a somewhat unique situation. Because of the interconnections, an innovation today encounters a set of patterns probably never encountered in the past. (Consider a declaration, admittedly ironic, on the Web site of Enron, once voted the United States' most innovative company for six years in a row by no less an authority than *Fortune* magazine: "Most of the things we do have never been done before.") This book will, I hope, offer advanced pattern-recognition skills to the slumbering game theorist in all of us, especially in preparation for the unfamiliar nature of innovation's journey.

STRATEGIC IMPLICATIONS: HOW THIS BOOK IS ORGANIZED

The contents of the chapters that follow unfold in two phases: the *why* of the slow pace of fast change and the *how*—creating a strategy for getting innovation to stick and have impact. The strategy will be guided by the considerations that arise in our framing of the why.

The why builds on the idea of equilibrium. Chapter 2 further develops the notion that an *inefficiency* is introduced by interconnection. As discussed, today's markets present innovations with barriers that arise from the realities of interconnectedness. An innovation's success in any kind of a market will ultimately hinge on the simple question of what drives adoption or the choices that favor adoption. In highly interconnected markets, such choices must be coordinated: adoption by one party will depend on adoption by others. Coordination by its very nature takes time.

Chapter 2 discusses the evidence for such inefficiency. It also explains that the root cause of the inefficiency is the fragmented and privately motivated form of decision making on which the innovation depends for market impact. Several different manifestations of the inefficiency and their causes are discussed.

Can we expect that the market will naturally evolve to a solution to this kind of problem, as it does with other kinds of inefficiencies? The odds are against a market solution. It will therefore be up to the innovator to design strategies to orchestrate a coordinated campaign across the network to bring about sustainable change and speed its pace.

Chapter 3 describes some of the basic items in the strategist's tool set, which will then be applied in the subsequent chapters. In other words, having explained the why, I then turn to the how. The object of strategy, in the current framework, is to unravel the equilibrium in the status quo and establish a new, favorable one.

This framing of the challenge has several implications:

1. Key to an innovation's success is the establishment of a new outcome in which choices are made in favor of its adoption. This future outcome needs to be qualified. This means that you must picture this outcome as an aggregation of player choices and then test the *plausibility* of these choices, as well as the desirability of the outcome. Then you must reason backward to ensure that the actions being taken on the path to that outcome are consistent with the objective of getting to such a target. There is a chicken-and-egg problem that needs to be resolved here: An innovator's early choices must anticipate the future, even while the choices are active in shaping that future.

2. A second key to an innovation's success is to break out of the status quo's gravitational orbit. Given the mutually reinforcing equilibrium that binds this status quo, innovators must orchestrate a coordinated attack

on it. Some mechanism must correlate the choices of multiple parties and propagate them further. This is the ballast necessary to get the innovation to the point of a critical mass of adoption. By itself, no innovator has infinite resources to intervene. It must find ways to create *selective* interventions that more strongly influence the rest of the system. The mechanism must, in other words, have a multiplier effect.

3. I emphasized earlier that innovators cannot, in general, expect to influence everyone on the network directly, despite the need for a coordinated attack. They will need allies—or agents—that create the leverage needed to exert influence on a wider group. Successful negotiation with such an agent and staying ahead of competitors aiming for similar access will be essential to getting to the final outcome. Managing this three-way interaction requires a tactical plan. As it turns out, the framework of equilibrium comes in handy even in making choices at this tactical level.

4. The trickiest part of strategy in fundamentally uncertain situations is that it is both about making some hard choices *and* about keeping options open. Making a choice concentrates resources on the most efficient path to the desired outcome and increases the chances of coordinating—and sometimes even limiting—the choices of others. On the other hand, the choices have to be based on an assessment of the various moving parts in the networked market environment. As a result, the outcome is uncertain, and any given player may not have complete confidence in its ability to steer toward a targeted equilibrium. This would suggest the need for criteria that will help an innovator decide when to make a firm, irreversible choice—a bet, really, given the uncertainty—and when to reserve the option to decide later with more

information in hand. It also raises the question of whether there are alternative ways of bridging a bet and an option, such as getting insurance, even for an up-front choice. All in all, an innovator needs to have a policy on how and to what degree it must *commit* to its strategic choices.

Chapters 4 through 7 build on these elements of strategy and offer practical frameworks for developing and deciding among the various ways to address each of these issues. Chapter 8 offers a conclusion and provides a frame for the reader to take the ideas of this book further and act on its broader interpretations.

A word on innovation: I am interested in the broadest possible definition. In the discussions to follow, innovation covers *new* products, technologies, business models, and other processes and ideas. It can even mean ways of organizing markets. As breaks from the status quo, all these innovations have the potential to add value in a market setting and contribute to what we would otherwise recognize as progress.

A concluding note: The examples in this book will focus on innovations in industries that are inherently information-intensive, since they produce the most intuitively apparent networks. Although the likes of IBM, Sony, Palm Computing, and several telecommunications players are discussed in the following pages, my conclusions are, by no means, limited to these industries. The only relevant criterion is whether an industry is, in my terms, *meaningfully* networked.

Consider, as an unusual suspect, the new sugar substitute sucralose, marketed under the brand name Splenda by Johnson & Johnson. Superficially, this product has little to do with a network, yet it too must contend with the kinds of interconnected markets that concern us. Its ability to penetrate the market to the point that its distinctive yellow packets sit side by side with the blue and pink packets of competing sugar substitutes on restaurant tables depends on a network.

This network includes the many early users who swear by the product and will spread the word to others, researchers who will conduct clinical studies to test it for long-term adverse effects, early adopter food manufacturers (such as Ocean Spray, Royal Crown Company, and the Velvet Ice Cream Company) that use it, and popular establishments such as Mc-Donald's or Starbucks that presently carry the blue and pink packets and will act as channels to the consumers.[20] In this sense, a new sugar substitute's ability to penetrate the market is as dependent on a connected world as is an innovation from IBM.

THE MAIN MESSAGE is that innovations and highly connected markets share a complex relationship: Everybody loves the idea behind a good innovation, but embraces it only when others embrace it as well.

Traditional strategy urges you to "Think Different." But thinking different is no longer sufficient for innovation's progress in a connected world. You need, instead, to "think equilibrium." This advice may not sound elegant or even grammatically correct. But I hope that the coming pages will convince you that it is, indeed, a rather beautiful idea.

Chapter Two

OF PAUSE AND PROGRESS

*We believe that a similar, nonlinear trend in
biotechnology capabilities is creating comparable growth
potential in the life sciences. . . . We believe that these genomic
technologies will continue to double in capability every 12 to
24 months—a statement we're calling "Monsanto's Law."*

—Monsanto Corporation, 1997 Annual Report

WE CAN ALL RELATE to discrete measurements of progress
from our own experiences. Many of us can remember times
when a fax machine was unknown. Others can remember the
first computer they bought for their homes. Another interesting place to watch the slow pace of fast change is on the wall
of new releases in the neighborhood Blockbuster store. The
slow incursion of the digital video disc (DVD) into the racks
of old-fashioned videotapes provides a visual diary of the pro-
gressive inroads of digitization. From when they first appeared on the scene, DVDs took a long time to even make a
tentative appearance on my local Blockbuster's wall. Once
they made their delayed entry, every other month their shelf
space seemed to spread further by a few inches. One day, the
wall will have no videotapes.

A New Mantra of Motion

Blockbuster's wall is a metaphor, but it is a limited one. Intel's cofounder, Gordon Moore, proposed a rule of thumb about the number of transistors that can be crammed onto a semiconductor chip. This so-called Moore's Law has become *the* metaphor for technological progress of our times. (The number, he predicted, would double every eighteen months.[1]) Futurists swore by it. Technologists saw in it their own law — an inevitable truth around which everyone could rally. Policy makers and venture capitalists had found a simple way of setting expectations for the steady upward curves of technology. It made optimists even of those engaged in dismal science. As Erik Brynjolfsson, of Massachusetts Institute of Technology (MIT), declared: "As long as Moore's Law continues, we should keep getting better off. It will make our children's lives better."[2] Without regard to industry boundaries, companies appropriated the law as a mantra guaranteeing rapid progress ahead. (Monsanto, however, is the only one I know of that put its own name against it as well.)

Given the central role of semiconductors as the brains of the information age, it is natural for Moore's Law to have had such a long reach. When viewed in the aggregate, the law creates expectations of increased productivity powered largely by innovations in information technologies.[3] The considerations raised in the previous chapter, however, lead us to question whether that technology's impact in the market actually matches the expectations. Remember, Moore's Law is about technological progress, not market adoption.

In fact, the pace of *realized* market progress is much slower than the blistering pace of technological progress suggested by Moore's Law. Although the improved processing power of computers may be resetting expectations about what new technologies can do for us, it is the processing power of the market that determines how fast those expectations ultimately get realized.

Therefore, I would propose that we need a corresponding "law" for realized progress: As a rule of thumb, technology's impact in the market will most likely proceed at only half the speed predicted by Moore. Inescapably, I must call this alternative mantra—if I may indulge in a final cinematic reference—demi-Moore's Law.

Like its inspiration, this law is meant more as metaphor than an exact metric. Its purpose is to focus on a paradox in markets with strong interconnections between their participants. The paradox is that these very interconnections create inefficiencies: Innovation is adopted at a slower pace—and often not adopted at all—*even though wider adoption would be almost universally beneficial*. As with the health-care system discussed in chapter 1, this slow adoption or lack thereof is because the affected market participants must dismantle a preexisting equilibrium and recoordinate a new one. As a result, the innovation takes longer to gain wide adoption and to have any impact. The delay in impact is beyond the diffusion delays one would naturally expect whenever an innovation is launched.

This outcome is inefficient when contrasted with an ideal situation in which the relevant network of players perfectly coordinates the changes in their behaviors necessary for adoption. In the ideal, most players would be better off than they would if the innovation were adopted inefficiently.

The ideal could come together in different ways. A critical mass of players could independently push for change, as in the example of digital imaging from chapter 1. Alternatively, a new outcome could be orchestrated, motivated, and even enforced by some central authority, as happens with many coordinated development programs in, say, China, Singapore, and parts of India. Finally, a single player or consortia with sufficient leverage—as in South Korea—could play a coordination role, although this role of coordinator has its limits when it triggers antitrust concerns. Of course, all these ideals are hard to come by in the decentralized, competitive markets that are the norm in the West. Hence, there is inefficiency. Since the cause of the inefficiency is in the interconnected structure of the market, I refer to it as *interconnection inefficiency*.

This chapter explores symptoms, and possibly evidence, for the inefficiency. It also explores the origins of inefficiency in different forms of networked market situations. We can reasonably ask if we should expect a market solution to the inefficiency. In other words, can some mechanisms close the gap between the expectation and the realization of an innovation's impact? I shall argue that the forces creating the inefficiency are likely to persist. Consequently, it will be up to the individual innovator to orchestrate a campaign to close or reduce the gap; the market will not heal by itself. Consider, first, an example highlighting the inefficiency.

Inefficiency: The Case of the 56K Pause

Most of us reach into the infinity of the Internet with the help of a simple, essentially invisible device: the modem. This tiny link commands a very powerful position in the information ecosystem. The modem's speed—that is, the number of bits of information it allows per second in and out of the computer—is arguably the most significant determinant of the quality of the Internet experience. The importance of the modem, of course, is of little surprise to those who have waited impatiently for an elaborately designed Web site to slowly come to life on a computer screen.

The relatively slow adoption of high-speed broadband modems has carried a disproportionate share of the blame for the slow pickup of a variety of information-rich content and service offerings, which so many players in telecommunications, the media, and Internet businesses have been planning for. There are precedents for the slow adoption of faster modems as modem speeds have increased over the years—these patterns tend to repeat in every generation. Perhaps less well known than the bottlenecks to broadband adoption was the slowdown involving the earlier generation of 56K modems.

The 56K modem, which could download information at the rate of fifty-six kilobytes per second, promised to double the speed of access relative to what was then the status quo in the fall of 1996. The outlook for adoption looked promising for several reasons. First, the demand for higher-speed modems was high and clearly left unsatisfied by the previous generation of products. Second, the 56K products did not cost much more than the older, slower variety. Finally, the benefits of higher speeds, apparent to anyone who used a PC to get online, were advertised widely. Despite this auspicious backdrop, a year after launch, the penetration rate of 56K modems had averaged a mere 20 percent. Surveys done in January 1998 showed that less than 50 percent of modems shipped were of this higher-speed variety.[4]

This rate of diffusion was much slower than expected, even after accounting for the normal lags in the adoption of new products. The effects of this slowdown lingered well past 1996. At the turn of the new millennium, many home computer users were still accessing the Internet at half the speed of a 56K modem. What happened?

The interconnected state of the market for modems provides clues toward an answer. Consider three elements relevant for adoption: customers, compatibility, and competition.

The primary customer for modems is a PC original equipment manufacturer (OEM), such as Hewlett-Packard, Dell, or IBM. Most modems are bundled with a PC. That is, OEMs physically install the modem of their choice into their computers so that when the individual consumer purchases the computer, the computer already has a modem installed. Some users, of course, buy individual PC components and assemble their own computer systems, but they represent a relatively small segment of consumers.

A 56K modem installed in a PC can download information at fifty-six kilobytes per second only when there is a 56K modem installed at the head-end in the network. This could be, for example, a server operated by an Internet service provider (ISP) conforming to the same standard as the one on the PC. If the modems at the two ends use incompatible standards, then the access speed drops, by default, to that of the older, slower modem.

Since the introduction of the faster modem, there were, primarily, two competing 56K standards: the X2 (sponsored by U.S. Robotics) and the K56Flex (sponsored by Rockwell Semiconductor). U.S. Robotics and modem manufacturers that used Rockwell as their supplier were competing head to head in the 56K market. Both were interested in establishing their own standard as the predominant one.

The market for 56K modems was a case study of a highly interconnected — or networked — market. In a networked market, the decisions of the various participants relevant for wider adoption of an innovation are closely linked to, and dependent on, each other. Moreover, the choices necessary for a switch to a new generation of modems are dispersed across several different parties, each of which has separate, private interests and constraints.

The network in this instance constituted several parties: the PC OEM, the user, the ISP, the two competing modem camps (U.S. Robotics and the manufacturers aligned with Rockwell), and others such as the PC distributors. Thanks to the competitiveness between the two standards, each participant had a critical binary choice. An OEM would select a particular 56K modem if it expected that its users also wanted such a modem. But users would want these modems only if they delivered on the promise of higher speed. The ability of users to achieve speeds of 56K was, in turn, predicated on which standard their ISP was favoring. The ISPs would, on their part, favor whichever standard they believed would assure them of the largest customer base; in other words, they would back the modem standard that most OEMs or PC distributors were likely to install in their machines. The outcome is that the market became a ring of interdependent decisions.[5]

Meanwhile, the modem competitors were engaged in a frenzy of activity to push the system toward coordination around their own standard. Through most of 1997, the modem market witnessed a race between U.S. Robotics and Rockwell to align the incentives of everyone in this ring in their favor.[6] Both sides were announcing deals that they had struck with major PC OEMs and ISPs. The public declarations of every deal were meant to be a signal to all others in the ring that because the signaling party was winning, everyone should move over to the winner's side and, by doing so, ensure victory.[7]

During this period, however, neither competitor emerged as a clear winner. Each decision maker, therefore, had to slow down and wait for a resolution. The cycle created a self-sustaining equilibrium, in which the older technology persisted longer than it should have, given the state-of-the-art engineering. As a result, customer experience remained tethered to the status quo. Access speeds remained — and for many, still are — well below fifty-six kilobytes per second, despite the superior products readily available. Technology created an expectation of progress that was not matched by its realization.[8]

Ironically, even before it hit the shelves, the 56K modem was already obsolete. New digital modem technologies — digital subscriber loop (DSL) and cable modems — promising speeds more than fifty times as fast were giving market participants further reason for pause. Part of the slowdown in the adoption of 56K modems could also be attributed to the expectation that an opportunity to leapfrog it altogether was within reach.

The slow uptake of faster modems is a particular illustration of the inefficiency of interconnection at work. It raises a broader question: Are there more widespread symptoms of inefficiency?

Wider Symptoms of Inefficiency

If we were to use a notion such as productivity as a measure of technology in use, or true progress, we may see wider evidence of demi-Moore's Law. In 1987, while the PC was becoming a common sight across the workplace, Robert Solow, an MIT Nobel laureate and growth theorist, had remarked, "We see the computer age everywhere except in the productivity statistics."[9] Back then, U.S. labor productivity (measured as output per hour in the nonfarm business sector) was growing at roughly 1.4 percent annually. Until 1995, Solow's quip continued to be on target, and the annual growth rate in productivity remained unchanged. Yet firms in the United States had made unprecedented levels of investment in information technology, which accounted for an estimated 30 percent of all new capital investment. This "productivity paradox" puzzled everyone concerned about the economic return on investment in information technology. To put it differently, considering the impact of Moore's Law on productivity, its bark seemed to have been louder than its byte.

Various explanations were offered to explain the paradox. Some focused on the possibility of inaccurate measurement; others, on the mismanagement of information technology spending. A separate school of information technology skeptics had doubts about the high expectations to begin with. One concern, for example, was that the Internet was not a first-order invention and that expectations of high productivity would be misplaced.[10] But then the numbers changed.

Since 1995, productivity statistics turned upward, with an annual average clip of 2.5 percent to 2.6 percent.[11] (Beyond the mid-1990s, productivity rose even further—at one point reaching the 4 percent mark—only to be readjusted back to around a 2.5 percent average, after some rechecking of the methodology.) This significant upward shift might suggest that the promise of technological progress was finally kicking in, but doing so much later than expected before settling into a new equilibrium.[12]

The inefficiency of interconnection offers an alternative explanation for the gap between expected and realized progress (as measured by the productivity statistics) as well as the stop-and-start pattern of realized progress. What the statistics reveal may be less of a paradox than a simple reflection of the difficulties of dismantling an old equilibrium both at an industry level and at a company level and getting the network participants to agree on new, compatible choices anchored around an innovation.

Although I have focused on the evidence from innovations in modern information technologies, the inefficiency associated with coordinating and recoordinating multiple decisions has been felt historically in network-based innovations of earlier generations as well. When the railways were introduced, it took time for businesses and factories previously located near waterways to relocate along railway lines. When modern machinery was introduced to England's textile mills in Lancashire or when electricity was introduced in factories, the necessity of redesigning or even tearing down entire buildings to accommodate the superior technology delayed adoption.[13] In both cases, coordination across the relevant network was a critical factor in the delay in creating market impact. Indeed, at the heart of the inefficiency is the networked market in which innovation must take root.

THE NETWORKED MARKET

The inefficiencies consistently arise because of networked markets, but the networks that interconnect participants in these markets arise in different ways. The markets that result do, however, have two characteristics in common:

- **Fragmented decision system:** The outcomes we observe in the market are the sum of many decisions. These decisions are spread across a wide group of market participants connected through one of several forms of networks.

- **Private initiative:** There is, generally speaking, no systemwide coordinator that enforces or directs individual choices. Even if the participants engage in a dialogue, the outcomes in networked markets are ultimately determined by private interests and constraints. This is to be expected in a typical private-enterprise system with competitive markets in which the decisions are made at an individual level. It is this individual or private rationality—rather than some consideration of the collective good—that determines market outcomes.

These characteristics—fragmented decision systems and private initiative—produce inefficiency. The decisions that make sense at the individual level are not necessarily the best choices when viewed in the aggregate. If, however, all parties were to switch in a coordinated way to an alternative outcome, they may all be better off. Coordinated change can have profound impact on an innovation's potential to penetrate and influence a market.

It is natural to ask, Why would an inferior outcome survive when there is a better alternative available? And what is to prevent the individual participants from switching to the alternative if they are made better off by doing so?

The answers lie in the dispersed, fragmented manner in which decisions are made in such markets. As a single participant, I make choices based on my expectations about the choices being made by others. The status quo may be in my best interest if I believe others are maintaining status-quo behavior as well. Each person's decision is justified from his or her own unilateral perspective, as well as the limited context and information with which that decision has to be made.

Inefficiency can take many forms, since networked markets can arise in many ways. The following sections will describe some of these forms.

Inefficiency Through Reliance on a Shared Resource

A network is created when many participants derive value from a common resource to which they have joint access. For example, a communications network is shared by many users.

To see how inefficiency can arise in such an environment,

consider a local area data network within a company. A common use of this resource is for company employees to send, receive, and store e-mail. The popularity of e-mail means that it is used more and more frequently for the communication of both trivial and critical information. There is so much e-mail that an employee has less time to read it. Consequently, users are loath to get rid of e-mail even after they have read it.

Psychologists theorize that, although there is gratification from sending or receiving e-mail, there is little gratification from having deleted it.[14] A company's employees store large volumes of e-mail in their electronic mailboxes, which takes up shared capacity on the corporate server. This electronic hoarding not only uses up space, but also potentially makes the network less efficient. It has real costs once the server is close to full capacity and additional capacity needs to be purchased. This raises costs to the entire firm and eventually adversely affects all users when the information technology manager must arbitrarily delete old mail to make space.

Fragmented decision making is evident in this environment: Whether to self-regulate is an individual choice dispersed among many employees—it is, typically, not one imposed by a central manager. Every employee makes the decision independently with the knowledge and assumptions available to that employee. Few feel strongly motivated to self-regulate and delete unnecessary e-mail, because none believes that unilateral action makes much difference to the overall situation. On the other hand, there is a clear cost to the employee in terms of time spent self-regulating and cleaning out old e-mail.

As a result, few employees are inclined to change their behavior. Although self-regulation by all is beneficial to the collective, it is not compatible with the incentives of the individual decision maker. An inferior status quo survives even though a commonly agreed-to and binding protocol involving self-regulation would, in the long term, benefit all.[15] Such "gridlock" can create barriers when an innovator attempts to introduce an innovation into environments with similar characteristics.

Inefficiency Through Complementary and
Competitive Interdependencies

A different way to think about a networked market is as an environment with interdependencies among parties that may be complementary or competitive—and sometimes both. Inefficiency may result when interdependent players are required to coordinate. Although consumers frequently make complementary buying decisions (as we observed in the case of the video-game console in chapter 1), the problem is especially acute when the complementary players also compete. This tends to happen more among firms.

Information-intensive products tend to have relationships that are complementary at some levels and competitive at others. This is because consumers combine several component products for different applications and derive value from their interoperability.

An example of such a relationship is the one between Microsoft and America Online (AOL).[16] These two behemoths compete in many areas: Internet service, instant messaging, portals, browsers, e-mail, Internet TV platforms, digital music, and so forth. More broadly, both are in pursuit of predominance in the evolving information industry. Their core sources of strength are different, even though each has a business that competes with the other's core. AOL dominates Internet service provision, and Microsoft dominates PC operating systems and applications software. From a consumer's standpoint, these products are complementary. For this reason, neither company can afford to ignore the benefits of interdependency with the other.

Traditionally, the Windows operating system used to come with AOL service, and AOL would use Microsoft's Internet Explorer as its default browser—even though each player has its own competing product. In particular, AOL's own browser, the Netscape navigator, was at the center of the landmark antitrust lawsuit against Microsoft.

Mutually beneficial agreements among such players are tenuous and constantly at risk of breaking down. Although some long-term collaboration within the bounds of antitrust regulations would benefit both companies and the industry and consumers at large, AOL and Microsoft are unilaterally motivated to break ranks. Each company refuses to commit to long-term cooperation with the other, which has resulted in several high-profile clashes between the two. Neither wants to play a role that might leave it subordinate to the other in future generations of Internet businesses.

For example, in the negotiations over linkages between the two on Microsoft's new generation of operating systems software, Windows XP, the two players clashed over the most contentious areas of competition between them: instant messaging and streaming media. The outcome is mutually harmful as it involves a slowdown in each company's ability to provide complementary services and bring innovative new products into wider use. Again, the outcome is dictated by unilateral interests and is at odds with the collective good. In markets dominated by such interdependent players, there is a considerable challenge in introducing innovations since they require motivators that align the disparate interests of each key player.

Inefficiencies Through Fragmentation in the Value Chains

An industry's value chain or value system comprises the various activities and products that combine to create an end product valued by consumers. Networked markets are created when the ownership of industry value chains gets subdivided among many different players with independent interests and ownership. In general, there has been a trend toward such fragmentation across industries.

Before the information age, many of the iconic players, who also set the tone for the rest of their industry, followed a significantly more integrated model of organizing their value chains. Ford, for example, not only exerted close control over all parts of its value chain and made its own auto parts, but once had its own rubber plantations to guarantee the supply, scheduling, and quality of its tires. In the pre-1980s mainframe computing industry, IBM produced all the essential components of the computer. The telecommunications industry was an integrated monopoly under the Bell System.

Times and business practices have changed. The advent of better means of transmitting information has led to greater fragmentation of the processes in the value chain. The examples of vertical integration just mentioned have all gone in the direction of dismantling their famously integrated structures. Ford and other automakers now rely on a hierarchy of suppliers, most of which do not even deal directly with the automakers.

Similarly, the seemingly indivisible IBM blew up its integrated model with Project Chess, its initiative to rapidly launch the IBM PC in the early 1980s. With the intention of getting to market quickly, IBM built its PC with a microprocessor from Intel, a power supply from Zenith, disk drives from the Tandon Corporation, printers from Epson, and, most famously, operating system software from a small start-up called Microsoft. This outsourcing and open-architecture model of organizing a value chain has spread throughout the industry.

The Bell System also went through a series of breakups that resulted in some fragmentation in the telecommunications industry. AT&T divested itself of local phone service in 1984 after the antitrust action brought against it. It then further divested itself of its equipment businesses. The remaining services company tried to reintegrate but then thought better of it and broke itself up further. The equipment company that was created, Lucent, went on to further separate into different businesses serving different market segments.

Besides such high-profile disintegration, there has been a long-term trend toward the splintering of value chains. Industry players retain core activities and outsource others deemed necessary but noncore. In each of these instances, the transformation in business practice has led to the creation of a networked market among different businesses and processes that must work together to create the final product. The resultant fragmentation of a firm's activities creates a potential coordination problem. Each player in these disaggregated value chains has private interests. Although their interests often do overlap, the players at each link compete for a larger share of the value created by the eventual sale to end users. Each player is under constant pressure to increase leverage to negotiate a better share.

Although some splintering of value-chain activities has been successful (think Cisco, Dell, or Wal-Mart) and can serve as role models for the rest, coordination remains a challenge. The separation of the decisions that must add up to a finished product introduces a potential for friction between the various partners. With this friction comes inefficiency. The problem of inefficiency is generally the most severe when there is no central coordinating player. Considered an ally by all, the coordinating player has invested in systems to make the fragmented structure work. Dell, for example, has done this with its tightly knit network of supply partners.

The sequel to the 56K gridlock discussed earlier provides an interesting vignette about how such inefficiency can play out. One of the principal forms of next-generation broadband modems is the DSL modem. Even if a customer were to decide to subscribe to DSL service, the wait would be far from over. Putting aside technical issues, the tangled value chain serving the customer partly explains the slow adoption of broadband, which has crippled the entire telecommunications industry.

In one common scenario, before many of the value-chain players went out of business, a web of several entities would serve the customer. He or she would order the service through an ISP, which, in turn, would turn the order over to a DSL provider, which would rely on a local phone company for access to phone lines.

Although DSL penetration is in the mutual interests of all these players over the long term, on any given account their interests do not coincide. If a customer orders DSL directly from a phone company, such as Verizon, then Verizon uses the same line to deliver phone and DSL service through a process of line sharing. If the order were placed through an ISP, however, Verizon is under no obligation to offer line sharing to the independent DSL provider to which the ISP has given the job. In this case, a second line would have to be run to the customer's home, which adds to cost and time. When the customer places a service call, the problem cannot be easily fixed, because of the interconnected nature of the delivery mechanism. Each player can justifiably blame some other player in the circle.

The result is this: The customer pays for broadband access with an inordinate expenditure of time, money, and mental anguish; fewer customers sign up; and all parties are hurt. Moreover, all of the players are trapped in their behavior because, within their localized context, they are making the best choice. This is yet another form of the challenge to the innovator attempting to penetrate a networked market.

Inefficiencies Through Connected Belief Systems

Less tangible forms of connection than the ones mentioned earlier also give rise to networked markets. These involve beliefs and expectations about critical market factors among otherwise independent decision makers. Such conditions arise often, particularly when there is uncertainty about the value that a product creates for the consumer.

Interdependent beliefs can arise in several different situations. They can be "manufactured" by marketing campaigns through powerful brands or through the positioning of products in the minds of consumers. The brand or the positioning becomes a standard, and a part of its credibility as a standard rests on each consumer's belief that others believe it as well. The objective of such campaigns is for a brand to become "sticky" and keep consumers from switching, even with superior alternatives available.

Interdependent beliefs also develop when market players seek benchmarks or look for analogies in markets with high uncertainty and little data to fall back on. The beliefs provide comparable assessments for making estimates and aid in pattern recognition or prediction.

Interdependent beliefs can lead to inefficiencies through over- or undervaluation of an uncertain factor. Market manias and crashes are the most extreme manifestations of such phenomena. For example, the speculative bubble that existed in capital markets before the spring of 2000 has often been described as a case of "irrational exuberance."[17] There is, in fact, a way to provide an internally consistent, rational explanation for such phenomena. Here is how the logic would run: Bubbles are aggregates of many mutually reinforcing, individual points of view. One believes in the virtue of, say, Internet pet food, as long as everybody else—entrepreneurs, investors, some early adopters—does so as well. Everyone adheres to similar beliefs because a symmetrical logic applies all around. The beliefs rationally reinforce each other and create seemingly irrational—read inefficient—outcomes.

How do such belief networks get started in the first place? Certain events become focal points around which beliefs begin to congeal. These events may be declarations by influential individuals or trends that circulate frequently and grab attention. Who can forget, for example, the focusing effect of the Queen of England getting new economy fever and dropping an investment of £100,000 into Getmapping.com, immediately triggering an investment frenzy in the United Kingdom?

A particularly dramatic illustration of benchmarking's leading to inefficiencies in belief networks comes from the auctions of 3G wireless communications licenses in Europe.

In the United Kingdom and Germany, for example, the public announcement of bids sent signals of the uncertain value of futuristic 3G services back and forth among the bidders—and the high bid kept rising. As long as the bids were rising, no bidder wanted to be left out of what was being signaled by others as a highly desirable opportunity. Before long, the bids in the auctions had spiraled to stratospheric levels.

While the outcome was a success in terms of initial revenue raised by the public authorities, it ultimately backfired. Every major winner had to cope with severe debt, which cast a pall over the industry and delayed the rollout of 3G.[18]

Finally, a network of beliefs is created when different generations of products or innovations are connected over time. For example, the previously discussed choices of video-game consoles and the adoption of the 56K modem faced time-based issues. Besides the here-and-now choice of which product is better, the affected parties also have to consider past products or future ones in their final decision. The consumer is unsure whether to make a commitment now or to wait until the next-generation option is available. Again, connected beliefs create inefficiency.

Consider the fate of the 3G services that were to have rolled out after the aforementioned auctions. One of the potential barriers to 3G adoption is the anticipation of an alternative technology, the wireless local area network (LAN), often referred to simply as 802.11, whose development has been growing at a very fast pace. The inexpensive deployment of LANs and their higher speed of access compared with equivalent 3G in fixed areas means that the uptake of 3G may suffer. At the opposite end, 3G may have competition from an earlier-generation 2.5G wireless communications service, which offers applications that are "good enough" for most mobile users. Such freezing between successive generations can create challenges for an innovation attempting to penetrate a market.[19]

FRAGMENTATION AND PRIVATE
INITIATIVE ARE HERE TO STAY

The basic characteristics of interconnected markets responsible for the inefficiency are the fragmentation of decision making and the motivation of decisions by private initiative. In a market-based system, private initiative has little likely alternative, other than some selective form of regulation. Might there be a market-based solution to the fragmentation? If there is such a solution, then our main concern about inefficiency in networked markets would be mitigated, and the innovator could breathe easier.

Unfortunately, the fragmented nature of the decision making is here to stay. Consumers tend to be widely dispersed and are, by definition, individually motivated decision makers, even if they were susceptible to influence from others. Better connectivity reaffirms the consumer's sense of independence and empowers autonomy in decisions.

On the firm's side, several factors reinforce an even greater dispersion of decision making.

- **Continuing spread of information technology and digitization:** Widening adoption of information technology reinforces the dispersion of decision making. It encourages a widening of the network by enabling more decision makers to be more effectively connected and potentially increasing the value to all members of the network.

- **Reduction in transactions costs:** Better information technology improves the flow of information between different firms in a value chain. One result of better information flow is lower transactions costs between businesses, which should make it easier to splinter the value chain or a firm's activities. This is consistent with the theory of the firm, originally developed by University of Chicago's Nobel laureate Ronald Coase: Transactions costs largely determine how far in its value chain or wider business environment an entity must exercise control, and where the market takes over. In other words, transactions costs drive the extent of integration of activities in firms.[20]

- **Increased pace of technological change and competitive innovation:** The pace of innovation itself acts as an impetus for fragmentation, through a division of labor and activities. Such division is often driven by the need to focus the deployment of resources to increasingly specialized aspects of R&D, technology, and product development, as well as the need to manage the costs of technology management more efficiently. Focus offers many advantages: technical depth needed to stay on the cutting edge; reduction of organizational conflicts between the innovative activity and incumbent businesses; improved cost management and better risk management by limiting investments to smaller bets.[21]

- **Wider acceptance of standards-based product development:** An important factor that has contributed to fragmentation on the supply side, at least in information-related industries, is the recognition of mutual gain in agreements on common standards. Standards-based product development allows a firm to develop its product with the knowledge that others can readily plug into it and improve on its functions or independently develop complementary products.

- **Better precedents for regulatory scrutiny:** Much like the antitrust action of an earlier era that dismantled the Bell System, the case against Microsoft has heightened the awareness among regulators of the potential for "value-chain creep" by dominant players and contributed to new guidelines. It has also helped mold the policy debate on antitrust in the context of networked markets whose products are intensive in information. This would contribute toward deterring the players' moves to integrate.

Network inefficiency is a potential barrier on an innovation's path to impact in connected markets, and an innovator ought not to expect a market solution to the inefficiency. It is, instead, up to the innovator to take the initiative to develop a campaign and get the innovation past these barriers toward wider adoption in the market.

INTERCONNECTION INEFFICIENCY: THE PRISONER'S DILEMMA IN A DIFFERENT GUISE?

The players in various networked markets appear to be prisoners of their own individualism. They would all be better off being bound to a coordinated set of moves to a new ideal outcome, but they do not have the incentive to make the necessary changes individually.

The imprisonment analogy is quite apt. It brings to mind a story, originally told in 1950 by Princeton mathematician A. W. Tucker, to illustrate the bifurcation between individual rationality and collective good. This is the well-known — and, unfortunately, overused — prisoner's dilemma. The notion has been influential in many connected decisions, from price wars to nuclear arms races.

While the original version of the story involves two parties, the basic elements of the dilemma are much more general. The problem facing the innovator attempting to enter a networked market contains elements of the prisoner's dilemma.

In the original, two prisoners are arrested and are connected by the jointly held knowledge of their crimes and misdemeanors. They would be better off colluding to keep mum and getting off, since the authorities have no other evidence. Interrogated separately, they are individually motivated to betray the other in the expectation of a reward for providing evidence. This is true no matter what they believe the other one is going to do. As a result, they end up with a mutually destructive outcome, in which each has ratted on the other and both are punished. Even with getting some concession for having told on the other, they are far worse off than had neither done so. The dilemma here is that they both would have been better off had they not said anything (the "ideal"), and yet their individual incentives preclude such an outcome.

In the markets that concern us, there are many prisoners. The dilemma giving rise to demi-Moore's Law has a similar gap between individual motivation and collective good. An important difference for us is that our purpose is to go beyond the interpretation of an existing situation. We instead ask, What strategies can an innovator adopt to resolve the dilemma or overcome it? The chapters to come establish such strategies as a source of market advantage.

The prisoner's dilemma is without question the single best-known problem in game theory. In the eyes of many, it is incorrectly equated with *all* of game theory. Having made the connection between the innovator's market problem and a central problem in game theory, it is only appropriate that we turn to the theory's tools to resolve the market issues.

I CLOSE THIS CHAPTER with a brief epilogue. I began with the story of the slow encroachment by DVDs on the shelves of Blockbuster. Armed with the framing of the issues in this chapter, you can speculate on the nature of the networked market that must have impeded the DVD's first appearance. Of the many participants of the network, one began as vapor and vanished into thin air after a few months of its brief appearance. A study by David Dranove of Northwestern University and Neil Gandal of University of California, Berkeley, and Tel Aviv University, suggests that preannouncement—or vaporware, as it is known in less polite circles—of the DIVX system by Circuit City slowed the adoption of the DVD.[22] Circuit City launched its system a full year after its preannouncement and abandoned it the following year.

Sometimes, it seems, even mere whispers can be responsible for putting progress on pause.

Chapter Three

A FRAMEWORK FOR

CONNECTED CHOICE

Chess is not a game. Chess is a well-defined form of computation. . . . Real life is not like that.

—John von Neumann, physicist,
computer scientist, and
father of modern game theory

IMAGINE THAT the participants in a networked market into which an innovation launches are players in a game. The strategist's role can then be said to be one of a game designer. The game board before the innovator is more complex than those with which we are generally familiar. Even the game of chess, which has had long service as cliché for business strategy, is simpler than what the innovator would be embarking on.

There are many players necessary for an innovation's success, not just the familiar two opponents in a chess game. Others who are not at the table at the start of the game may even enter when the opportunity arises. The relationships between the players are complicated, and the players are connected through one of the various kinds of networks discussed in chapter 2. Some players may not even be considered opponents, unlike the classic black versus white in a chess game; others, such as Microsoft and AOL, are both complementary and competitive. The rules of the game are not all hard and fast. Some rules can be changed midgame by the players. Nor are all the moves visible; different players have access to different information and have different motivations.

Although chess is generally considered a particularly difficult game to play, the game of innovation is far more daunting still. And here is where a disciplined framework, such as game theory, is helpful.

The first purpose of such a framework is not necessarily to predict the right answer, but to make sure that we are asking the right questions. Nevertheless, it is critical to move beyond questions to actions that move an innovator toward its market objectives. The second purpose is to provide tools that serve in three capacities: to frame the key issues, to connect them with the various levers available to the strategist, and to present decision criteria to facilitate choices among these levers in a campaign to take innovation to market. This chapter aims to set up these questions and to introduce the main tools.

STRATEGY QUESTIONS

In framing the basic problem of bringing an innovation to market, an innovator should consider the following key questions. These questions are interrelated; together, they establish the ground rules for an innovator's campaign.

Who Are the Players on the Critical Path to the Innovation's Adoption?

Players can range from individual decision makers to organizations that make executive decisions to broad categories or segments that have shared characteristics and similar factors affecting their choices. On the supply side, they include market participants in the value chain with inputs into the innovation; those with enabling technologies and products; those that act as distributors to the players on the demand side; those that control the rules of the market by regulating it or establishing laws for it; and those with competing technologies and products that might otherwise constrain the innovation's progress. On the demand side, the player set includes the various consumer segments that constitute possible targets for the innovation and those whose consumption can influence others on the demand side.

As discussed, because the decision system can be fragmented, there may be many players to consider. These players must be prioritized according to their relevance to the innovation's success. We must, in addition, understand the linkages between the ones considered the most important along the critical path to adoption.

What Is the Nature of the Status Quo to Be Unraveled?

The purpose here is to understand the situation that the innovation intends to change. We must be able to describe it in terms of choices or behaviors of each player just specified. If this situation resists change, we must understand the aspects of the different players' choices that reinforce each other and lock in the status quo.

What Must Happen for a New Outcome to Be Created?

A departure from the status quo is assured only when a critical mass of the players changes behavior. Beyond this point, further changes occur on their own momentum. For the changes to survive, the new set of choices must be mutually reinforcing and lock into a path to wider adoption of the innovation.

What Are the Innovator's Levers?

The answers to the earlier question help set up the target choices or behaviors of players on the innovation's critical path. We now have a goal for the innovator's strategy. The strategy must be to orchestrate the many behavior changes away from the status quo to a new point of recoordination. Activating such a strategy requires an understanding of the underlying factors that govern each player's choices. Some of these factors help drive players toward the new outcome; others act as constraints. Several of these factors derive, in turn, from the choices being made by other players on the network. An understanding of these factors and the relationships between the players helps establish the feasibility of getting to the new outcome. It also helps pinpoint where the innovator must selectively look for levers to move the system.

How the Music Industry Went from Pause to Fast Forward, Part 1

To see how the preceding key questions establish the ground rules for an innovator's campaign, consider an example from the music industry. Among the most celebrated of the tiny group of heroes that emerged from the first wave of the Internet revolution was a company that made no money. While that was not abnormal for the time, this company was a hero of questionable legal status. It was almost saved by one of its biggest competitors, but eventually went belly up. What it did achieve, however, was the shake-up of one of the most remarkably sturdy examples of the status quo in any industry.

The company in question is Napster. It had targeted the status quo in the recorded music industry—one whose stability had few parallels. For proof of this stability, consider the price of a CD when the format was in its infancy: around fifteen to seventeen dollars per CD. We still pay about that much. It may be only the quality of new music that is on the decline.

A second aspect of the status quo has proved equally enduring. Music comes bundled in indivisible packages of tracks. Usually, only some of them are ones that a buyer really wants to hear. Since the mid-1980s, the package of choice has been the CD. In an environment in which practically all other consumer products experience both price declines and customization from competitive or innovation pressures, this was a recipe for a disruption waiting to happen.

Napster's arrival demonstrated a way in which such a disruption would be achievable. Users could freely swap unbundled digital music files from each other's computers through Napster's peer-to-peer file-sharing system. This disruption left much business unfinished in getting the innovation to stick. It had surfaced a crucial question: Now that technology had opened the door, how could it be leveraged into a viable business model for distributing recorded music with unbundled tracks with fair pricing and continue to promote creativity? Such a model would motivate the relevant market players to make the choices necessary for the new system to survive and thrive.

Finding answers to the preceding question means being able to answer questions such as these: Who are the players critical to the success of such an innovation, since they will be crucial to the business model? Why was the music industry's status quo so durable? How will that durability act as a barrier to the innovation's progress in the market? What conditions would lead to a new equilibrium in which the innovation produces a new music-distribution environment of unbundling and fair pricing? What are the potential levers for a successor to Napster (or for one of the keepers of the status quo interested in business model innovation) to influence the nature of that new equilibrium and to make it happen?

BREAKING DOWN THE MARKET INTO ITS FUNDAMENTAL UNITS

The fundamental units of the market are the players and the choices they make. In the following sections, we will look specifically at the choices and how they relate to innovation.

To understand this relationship, we must understand two issues: (1) choice factors, that is, the drivers governing the choice, and (2) the necessary conditions for a stable and mutually reinforcing market outcome: equilibrium.

Choice Factors: The Private Drivers That Govern a Player's Choices

The decision maker in the status quo and in the future equilibrium is a player whose choices depend on several underlying factors. These factors help explain the gap between the two outcomes. Also, given the interconnection among the players, the factors that affect one player's choices are often linked to the choices of others.

These choice factors can be organized in many ways. From the standpoint of actionable implications, it is most helpful to identify them by whether they help or hinder a player's inclination to switch from the status quo toward the new outcome. In other words, these factors both *motivate* and *constrain* the player.

Furthermore, an innovator must understand how it can influence these positive and negative factors. There are two additional ways in which the innovator can parse the information on motivators and constraints to find levers. First, the innovator must clearly know which factors are hard data and part of the player's observable context and which are perceptions. Second, an innovator should distinguish the factors related to the other network players and those originating from forces outside the network. This distinction yields insight into the channels through which the innovator can seek to influence these players. Table 3-1 presents a further breakdown of the factors and the innovator's levers.

A player's choices derive from a combination of the factors shown in the table. Moreover, these factors and how they

TABLE 3-1

A Player's Choice Factors and the Innovator's Levers

Source of Factor	Observable Factors	Perceived Factors
Other Network Players' Actions	Levers created by influencing network players to take actions observable to the player	Levers created by marketing and informational initiatives or through signals from other players
Factors Outside the Network	Levers created by causing changes in broader external events or systemic trends verifiable by the player	Levers created by marketing and informational initiatives

drive choices can be analyzed through research and informed conjecture. The advantage of understanding player choices by understanding the underlying choice factors is that it helps not only with an explanation and anticipation of player behavior, but also with finding levers to actively influence them.

Equilibrium: The Outcome That Results from the Players' Choices

The strategist has a two-part objective: unravel a status quo and orchestrate a new outcome that recoordinates the choices of several players. Both end points can be described through a single framework: the notion of equilibrium. A consideration of equilibrium is useful for diagnosing why the status quo is locked in. It is also a tool for testing if the target outcome under consideration will be sustainable. Equilibrium, in essence, is a consistency check on the story we tell to describe the behaviors of the players at crucial stages of the game.

How do we identify when a market is in equilibrium? We need to consistently apply a best-choice principle to each of the key players' behaviors and decisions, given the options available to a player. This approach to the definition was a key insight of John Nash, who demonstrated that any game under a reasonable set of conditions has at least one such equilibrium outcome.[1]

I modify my application of his original idea to focus on its actionable implications and place it in a market context. First, what is best for a given player will be determined by the underlying choice factors for the player. Additionally, three tests help identify if a situation (either present or future) is, or will be, in equilibrium.

> **Demand-side best choice:** When a market is in equilibrium, the demand behaviors—including those involving purchase and usage—are relatively stable and unchanging. From the available options, each buyer or user is making the best choice in response to what is known and expected about the following:
>
> - The competing alternatives to the innovation
> - The alternatives available from providers of complementary and enabling products
> - The choices being made by other buyers and users in the same networked market
> - How these factors will change in the future
>
> **Supply-side best choice:** In equilibrium, the choices of firms that compete with or complement the innovation have little or no impact on demand-side behavior. These choices are relatively stable and unchanging, for any of the following reasons:
>
> - No firm wants to change unilaterally, given each firm's expectations of what the others are doing.
> - Any change by a single firm is effectively neutralized, in terms of meaningful impact on purchase and usage, by a response from another player.

- Any change in strategy by any single firm is too small to have an impact, leaving the expectations and behaviors of all others unchanged.

- Demand-side behaviors are unaffected because of preexisting constraints within the demand context, and the strategies of the firms have no effect on these constraints.

Believability: The behavior being tested for its equilibrium characteristics must be believable from the innovation strategist's perspective, given the available data and hypotheses about each key player's choice factors. Any behavior considered part of an equilibrium must be consistent with the data or the most plausible hypotheses about these players' choice factors.

If these three tests are met, the behaviors of the various key players have locked into a self-reinforcing configuration. If everyone on the network were making a best choice, then there would be no unilateral motivation to switch to something new.

How the Music Industry Went from Pause to Fast Forward, Part 2

The frameworks just given—the choice factors and the definition of equilibrium conditions—are ways of capturing the essential drivers behind an interconnected market's response to innovation. In this example from the music industry, I use these frameworks as broad guidelines for telling an intuitive story about the players that make up a market. The frameworks just outlined can also be useful in shepherding *any* product through a market, of course. The biggest challenge for an innovation is that it must displace a preexisting equilibrium

and establish its own. That is why these frameworks are particularly powerful in the current context.

The Players

Consider again the players and the nature of the status quo in
the music industry. Following the definition of equilibrium conditions, I will organize the dramatis personae into two broad
groups. Most groups (record labels, artists, retail outlets, etc.)
fall on the supply side, whereas one group—the consumers—
falls on the demand side. In the process, I examine the choice
factors and the equilibrium conditions just presented.

Record Labels

Of the U.S. recorded music industry, 85 percent is shared
by five large conglomerates or their record label arms: Sony,
Vivendi Universal, EMI Group, Bertelsmann, and AOL Time
Warner. More than 50 percent of the price paid for a CD goes
to the record label. This market power alone is an important
consideration in determining what motivates the labels.

The labels' extraordinary power has several origins. When
a label signs up an artist, it has ownership of copyright over the
content. Being part of a major conglomerate gives each label
enormous marketing and distribution reach. Also, with only a
handful of labels, they are relatively well matched and each is
expected to act consistently in dealings with other players.

The labels are motivated by their corporate objectives and
the constraints just described; each has expectations that the
remaining four will be guided by roughly similar considerations. Implicit in these expectations is that any break from the
"standard" would result in a disruptive cycle of uncertainty
that could hurt everyone. No single label has an incentive to
lower prices, for example; all believe that the other labels are
also similarly disinclined. As a result, a status-quo equilibrium
is maintained, with little motivation to rock the boat.[2]

Given the extent of their control, the labels themselves can help explain the robustness of the music industry status quo. Besides them, however, there are other members of the supporting cast whose best-choice responses to the labels also help in reinforcing this situation. These players are described in the following paragraphs.

Music Retail Stores

This group includes several categories of players: specialists, such as Tower Records; general electronics and entertainment retailers, such as Best Buy; and the mega-generalists, such as Wal-Mart. Although most retail stores have limited ability to influence the overall equilibrium, some, such as Wal-Mart, are powerful in setting terms and even in setting limits on the music they are willing to stock. None is motivated to lead a fundamental disruption in the status quo, since they fear that the primary form of such disruption would be in the way music is distributed. They worry that if distribution were disrupted, they might no longer serve as intermediaries. Their interest in preserving the status quo is a best choice.

Artists, Publishers, and Songwriters

This community originates the content. The sale of the content generates revenues to several of these stakeholders, depending on how the music is used. The artists and songwriters would conceivably be of two minds about the question of status quo versus an uncertain future alternative with lower prices and unbundling of tracks. On the one hand, the labels retain a disproportionate share of the value created and dictate the terms to the rest of the industry. This would act as a motivator to the artists, publishers, and songwriters to look for alternatives to the status quo. On the other hand, many artists whose music is in demand owe their success to the very power and marketing muscle of the labels, which would make the artists think twice about disturbing the present situation despite the inequity.

To further complicate matters, several unresolved issues in the alternative means of distributing and packaging music would act as a constraint on the artists—by introducing some nervousness in their beliefs about switching from status quo. The spread of free and unregulated file-sharing systems such as Napster, or its successors such as KaZaA, was perceived by many artists as a threat to their revenue streams. Second, the lack of resolution on the management of digital rights—which would, in turn, affect how revenue is shared—was also a source of nervousness for this community. To summarize, this group apparently would not have the motivation to independently go out of its way to break the status quo unless a clearly superior—and stable—alternative were in sight.

Consumers

This key set of players falls on the demand side of the equation. Consumers are motivated by their desire to listen to music they enjoy and are constrained by the price of purchasing the music package as well as their inability, historically, to unbundle the package. In addition, a key motivator for many buyers of music is ownership and control of a music collection that matches their personal tastes.

Prior to alternatives such as Napster, most music buyers had few options to combine their desires to listen to music, enjoy the breadth of a collection, and have a collection of their own—other than to buy from the labels. Making copies was cumbersome, and the quality was not always as good as the original. For consumers, it was a best choice to support the status quo, given the options on the supply side.

A NEW LOOK AT DEMAND-SIDE
AND SUPPLY-SIDE PLAYERS

The consumers' behavior on the demand side could be construed as a best response to the behaviors on the supply side. For its part, the supply-side behavior is also consistent: a best choice of proceeding cautiously, given the hesitant demand for any change from status quo from consumers. All these factors would contribute to a lock-in of status-quo behaviors.

It was this self-reinforcing equilibrium that Napster managed to break. The path Napster took to reach this break-in is interesting. The first step was to change the status-quo choices on the demand side. These changes can be traced to the motivators just listed. Napster offered consumers access to music for free, as an alternative to the labels and the retail stores; it offered a wide range, making it anything but cumbersome to transfer the music files, especially in dorm rooms with high-speed Internet access (where one of the biggest audiences for Napster was resident). In addition, the company gave consumers an appealing sense of a collection, albeit on their hard drives instead of their shelves — quite desirable to the target audience. This appeal across the key adopter segments gave Napster its leverage points.

Interestingly, for a brief period before its operations were halted by the courts, Napster could create its own new equilibrium by transforming demand-side players into the supply-side players through its peer-to-peer file-sharing plan. The traditional supply-side players could be shut out. In other words, the similarly motivated consumers could maintain a self-contained equilibrium entirely by making a best choice to trade with each other.

This equilibrium-sustaining capability gave Napster its strength and led to a serious reconsideration of the status quo by the traditional supply-side players, particularly the music labels. The problem could not be resolved simply by bringing legal constraints on Napster; other players were emerging with similar capabilities to create an equilibrium where the supply and the demand sides of the market were "peer-to-peer."[3]

Note that in establishing its new, temporary equilibrium, Napster had changed the set of players critical to the innovation relative to the set that had held the status quo together. But what about the new equilibrium, a more sustainable innovation where music can be unbundled and purchased at a fair price within the bounds of a viable business model? This new business model would compensate all the relevant players and sustain an industry, even if it is a completely restructured one.

If the prime mover behind the new equilibrium were a major music label, several aspects of the path to the new equilibrium had to be clarified. First, the supply-side players being shut out by the Napster equilibrium would be inclined to look for a viable business model in a new, post-Napster equilibrium in which their respective interests are met. At the very minimum, the labels would seek to retain the rights to the content and earn a fair price for transferring a digital file to the consumer. They would not want the consumer to have the capability to reproduce it with ease and transfer it free of cost to others. This, at a minimum, was what had to true for the new equilibrium to sustain and satisfy the mutual best-choice criteria on the supply side.

Checking the best-choice criteria across the key players helps qualify this equilibrium: The minimal conditions must be plausible, and the outcome must still favor the innovating player. Once the outcome is qualified, the innovator must devise a mechanism to get from status quo to that outcome. The mechanism must suggest the different levers that generate simultaneous changes in behaviors among the network of players necessary for the new equilibrium to come together.

Perhaps this mechanism would need a new set of players. In the course of groping toward a new equilibrium, the music industry has spawned a new set on the supply side. Two separate coalitions among the music labels, MusicNet (BMG, EMI, and AOL Music) and pressplay (Sony and Vivendi Universal) have formed to distribute music files over the Internet. New technology partners, RealNetworks (for MusicNet) and Microsoft (for pressplay), have become essential to these markets.

Next, certain players may play a pivotal role in getting behaviors to change across a fragmented network of participants. With relationships, technologies, or brands that allow broad access, these players would act as agents of influence in the wider network. One such player—given its brand recognition with customers and its technology—was deemed to be Napster itself. Realizing this potential to offer such critical access, Bertelsmann broke ranks with the other labels and made an offer to acquire Napster's assets.[4]

Finally, in choosing to target a particular endgame, the innovator does so in a context of uncertainty. There would be several reasons for uncertainty about the path to the endgame. In retrospect, we can go over a long list of issues that these initiatives have had to confront. But even in advance, an innovator could expect many difficulties. For example, for a while it seemed that the two online music coalitions would have exclusive rights to different sets of artists. While one owns rights to the likes of Michael Jackson, Aerosmith, and Limp Bizkit, the other has Britney Spears, Madonna, and 'N Sync in its corner. This partitioning would be unappealing to the consumer who wants easy access to both sets. The division could also potentially turn consumers away from both the MusicNet and the pressplay sites. With two fiercely competitive technology partners, RealNetworks and Microsoft, on either side, it would be challenging for the two coalitions to pool their resources.[5] And then there would be uncertainty about an outcome sufficiently restrictive to prevent consumers from reproducing the music they obtain online.

With these and other risks in view, the innovator must decide how much and in what form to commit up front to a specific strategy for establishing a new equilibrium. Should, say, BMG put all its online efforts into MusicNet, or should it plan on other backup options? Alternatively, would it make sense to continue efforts to defend the status quo in the hope that, like many new-economy threats, this one too would pass?

My purpose here is not to answer these industry-specific questions, of course. Instead it is to highlight the following fundamental aspects of a strategy campaign for getting innovation to market in a connected world:

- Qualifying a winning endgame that the alternative strategies are designed to create and thereby making current strategic choices

- Establishing a mechanism that can help spread an innovator's influence across the potentially fragmented network of players on the critical path

- Actively managing the tactics of the interactions with the few pivotal players to focus on who will then influence the rest of the network

- Deciding on the degree and form of commitment to make, given that the strategic choices have to be made in a highly uncertain environment

Each of these aspects of strategy is an outcome of taking a game-theory mind-set on the issues before us. Each is an aspect of a campaign to take innovation to connected markets and the subject of chapters 4, 5, 6, and 7.

Chapter Four

BEGINNING AT THE ENDGAME

"Would you please tell me which way I ought to go from here?"
"That depends a good deal on where you
want to get to," said the Cat.

—Lewis Carroll, *Alice's Adventures in Wonderland*

AN INTERCONNECTED MARKET can take an innovation in different directions, many of which are hard to control or even connect to the starting point. Mark Twain saw his first Remington typewriter in a Boston dealer's window, walked in, watched a demonstration of a woman typing seventy-five words a minute, and instantly bought the machine. Targeted at lawyers, writers, and clergymen—who took pride in exquisite penmanship—Christopher Latham Sholes' writing innovation did not catch on despite the famous early adopter. It took the advent of the telephone, the telegraph, and the railways and the depersonalization and spreading out of businesses after the Civil War to create the right environment for what the *Penman's Art Journal* in 1887 described as the "monotonous click" to be heard in businesses around the United States.[1] Only after the typewritten word became more widely visible and acceptable and after the economies of scale lowered the prices did lawyers, writers, and clergymen go out and follow the lead of Mark Twain.

From a strategic viewpoint, choosing from among the many paths leading out of the point of launch and guessing where the interconnections might lead can make one's head hurt. This is especially true when one considers that the direction one takes could shape the future outcome, much as the large-scale purchases of typewriters by business users brought prices down for others. Also, working forward from the current state of knowledge may not help an innovator figure out which path to take. Should the next generation of wireless applications providers, for example, aim for hot spots such as the Starbucks outlets and hotel lobbies or warehouses and factory floors? The tendency is to look back into the past, bolster with market research the understanding of a market that does not currently exist, and then push ahead. I propose, instead, to turn this thinking on its head: Begin with an endgame, and only then work back to current choices.

By *endgame*, I mean three things:

- A forward-looking view of the targeted market outcome described in terms of the choices of the players whose interconnections actually give rise to the outcome.

- A stable view of the future, even if it is temporary and is replaced after some period of stability. This is the view once the innovation has launched, the players have reacted and adjusted to the choices of others, and an internal momentum among the choices reinforces the innovation's adoption. In other words, the endgame is the view after the choices have crossed a threshold of critical mass.

- A future that can be shaped by the choices the innovator makes along the way.

Our discussion thus far has been about the *why* of the slow pace of fast change. Much of the focus has been the status quo.

Now, as we turn to the *how* part of the discussion, I take the future, the endgame, as the initial point of focus.

The endgame is shaped by current choices; at the same time, current choices are dependent on the endgame being targeted. Think of M. C. Escher's famous lithograph *Drawing Hands*, of two hands, each drawing the other. In the interconnected market, the current set of choices is one hand; the endgame is the other. This, naturally, raises the question, Which hand do we begin with?

Imagine yourself in a position of having to make a strategic choice from among several options. It is common to make a guess about where the strategy will lead and then to act on that guess. A principle of reasoning back from the endgame suggests that, before making a choice on how to act today, you should make sure your guess about the targeted future is consistent with what you know to be true today. These are the most plausible futures, from which you must pick one—a preferred endgame—to target.

Sound simple enough? You may be surprised at how hard it can be to follow through on this apparently innocuous idea. Consider the case of the thirty-thousand-cell Excel model of world domination, which helps explain why working back from the endgame leads to better outcomes than does reasoning the other way around.

THE THIRTY-THOUSAND-CELL EXCEL MODEL OF WORLD DOMINATION

In the late 1990s, we were advising a prominent player in communications technology on the choices it was considering about how to enter a market with an innovation. Several details of the actual experience have been simplified to highlight the main point, but the fundamental strategic elements in the situation described on the following pages are true to the original.

The client, let us call it DominaCom, was planning an entry into a new market segment. The market was being served by a powerful incumbent with a product based on an earlier generation of technology. DominaCom had some options to think through along two dimensions. First, there were two possible technologies available to create the innovation: To keep matters simple, let us call them a Highbrow option and a Middlebrow option. Highbrow had a greater customer-value potential, but was also more expensive. A second key aspect of the choice was timing. It had become quite clear that the incumbent was not going to be sitting on its hands but was planning a competing upgrade of its own product, by applying either the Highbrow or the Middlebrow technology. The incumbent could carry out the upgrade preemptively if DominaCom were to delay its entry long enough but showed a clear intent to enter. Alternatively, the competitor's upgrade could occur as a reaction to DominaCom's entry.

What was DominaCom to do? Choose Highbrow or Middlebrow? Move first, or demonstrate intent to enter and move second? There was a major presentation to senior management in the offing, and commitments of large sums of money hung in balance. A high-powered task force, assigned to study the matter, returned with a highly sophisticated model fed by enough data and calculations to boggle the most formidable of minds. The model had crunched through the numbers and had reached a verdict: Pick Highbrow, and move first.

What if the incumbent came back with its own technology upgrade? Would that change the numbers? Would it not make sense to wait and see what the competitor did and then move and, in the meantime, make irreversible commitments to enter the market anyway? Never mind, said the model. Its conclusions were even more startling. Highbrow trumps Middlebrow, *no matter what the competition does*.

The model could not lie: It had thirty thousand cells in Excel, claimed its authors. Table 4-1 summarizes the numbers (which represent the net present value associated with the strategy, or NPV) that the thirty thousand cells added up to.

TABLE 4-1

Payoffs to DominaCom (NPV)

	If Competitor Chooses Highbrow	If Competitor Chooses Middlebrow
If DominaCom Chooses Highbrow	$3.5 billion	$6.5 billion
If DominaCom Chooses Middlebrow	$2.0 billion	$5.0 billion

As the table quite clearly reveals, DominaCom had in Highbrow that elusive—almost divine—solution to the most knotty strategy problem, a scenario-independent strategy. This strategic choice trumps the other option in any scenario, regardless of what the competition chooses to do. In both columns in the table, the NPVs yielded by Highbrow are higher. The model used publicly available data sources and market analysis. Its conclusions were in line with what an intuitive understanding of the industry economics would suggest as well. If the competition were to conduct an independent analysis of DominaCom's motives, it would certainly reach the same conclusion: Highbrow would be a dominant choice for DominaCom in either scenario.

Yet, not everyone in the strategic decision-making group was prepared to forge ahead with Highbrow. The more conservative ones argued that, although the model was quite compelling, it would make sense to show intent to enter and wait and see what the incumbent picked; DominaCom always had the option of picking Highbrow anyway. Waiting did not significantly change the financials given in the table, and the certainty of knowing what the competition would do would more than compensate for the delay.

At this point in the stalemate, a third group argued for a bridging solution: Examine the competitor's motivations.

Assuming that the competitor was driven by similar considerations, in other words, maximizing its NPV, this would translate into an inquiry into what the financials would look like from the incumbent's perspective.

To all these alternative proposals, the model's authors still had an apparently watertight response: The model is a good one, and it says the competitor's choice does not matter. Highbrow is the dominant choice, no matter what we learn about the competitor.

What do you think? Try reflecting on the issues before reading further.

As will be discussed in the following pages, there is more to this problem than meets the eye. Consider again the choices before DominaCom, and also visualize their possible alternative future outcomes. In the present context, this is not hard since there are only two players, and their strategic options are simple (for DominaCom: move first or move second, choose Highbrow or choose Middlebrow; for the competitor: choose Highbrow or choose Middlebrow).

DominaCom's decision can be envisioned in several stages. Initially, it must choose between moving first and moving second.

Suppose it were to decide to go *first*. In this case, there are four alternative paths to the endgame:

1. DominaCom chooses Highbrow, then the Competitor chooses Highbrow.

2. DominaCom chooses Highbrow, then the Competitor chooses Middlebrow.

3. DominaCom chooses Middlebrow, then the Competitor chooses Highbrow.

4. DominaCom chooses Middlebrow, then the Competitor chooses Middlebrow.

There is an alternate path, however. Suppose DominaCom were to decide initially to move second. In this case, there would be four alternative paths to the endgame, where the order of the moves listed above is reversed (e.g., the competitor chooses Highbrow, then DominaCom chooses Highbrow).

How does DominaCom's choice depend on thinking through the alternative outcomes that could result after these different paths play out? Here is how reasoning back from the endgame provides a guide. First, assume a decision has been made in the first stage, and ask what DominaCom would anticipate for the subsequent stages of play. In other words, ask which outcomes are plausible in the second stage. The answer to this plausibility question must, however, be given by taking this reasoning process one step further. Assume a decision has been made in the second stage, and anticipate what is the most plausible outcome in the third, and final, stage. In each case, the decision made at any stage is predicated on decisions anticipated in the stage ahead. DominaCom's choice in the first stage, to move first or to move second, must be based on working back from a targeted endgame, which is the most preferred one (i.e., the outcome with the highest NPV) on the short list of plausible outcomes.

This raises the issue of how to gauge plausibility. Since the outcomes depend entirely on the choices of the two players, plausibility is directly related to the choice factors that motivate and constrain each player. With the data in the table and the sequence of play, we have the relevant information for DominaCom's choice factors. We need the competitor's corresponding numbers to complete the picture.

The argument thus far had been that an assessment of the competitor's financials was unnecessary, because DominaCom's Highbrow strategy was dominant. Suppose, as an experiment, we were to estimate the financial impact to the competitor in each of these scenarios. In reality, a few hundred cells of additional analysis to the existing thirty thousand yielded the following important conclusion: *The competition is always better off matching whatever technology our client chose.* This is captured in table 4-2 by the directionally correct payoffs in NPVs to the competitor.

Armed with this information about the competitor, now consider alternative options before DominaCom (table 4-3). Thus, reasoning back from the future yields a surprising result. The original recommendation of the task force that seemed to be unambiguously the right choice is the last one on the list of plausible endgames. The best decision, as it turns out, is to move first and then choose Middlebrow.

TABLE 4-2

Payoffs to the Competitor (NPV)

	If Competitor Chooses Highbrow	If Competitor Chooses Middlebrow
If DominaCom Chooses Highbrow	$3.0 billion	$2.0 billion
If DominaCom Chooses Middlebrow	$2.0 billion	$3.0 billion

TABLE 4-3

DominaCom's Options and Consideration of the Endgames

DominaCom's Options	What Endgame Would Result from This Choice	DominaCom's Payoff in the Endgame
Move first, then choose Highbrow.	In the last stage, the competitor would match DominaCom's technology and choose Highbrow as well.	From table 4-1, this choice would result in $3.5 billion in NPV.
Move first, then choose Middlebrow.	The competitor would match DominaCom's technology and choose Middlebrow as well.	From table 4-1, this choice would result in $5 billion in NPV.
Move second.	DominaCom will choose Highbrow in the final stage since the competitor has already made its choice by the time it gets to choose. Anticipating this endgame outcome, the competitor would choose Highbrow itself since it is motivated to match DominaCom's technology.	From table 4-1, this choice would result in $3.5 billion in NPV, with some added benefit from the certainty of knowing the competitor's choice.

QUALIFYING THE ENDGAME

Working back from a targeted future clearly proved to be of benefit to DominaCom. More generally, we need a process for qualifying the multiple futures that can be imagined at the start of an innovator's campaign. We have seen an illustration of qualifying the future in relatively simple situations in the last example, in which there were two players, each with a few options. Endgame reasoning suggests a way to extend such a process to situations with more players in a more fragmented network.

First, consider your strategic options at any point in time in the campaign, and mentally play them out as far as you can to all possible endgames. Base these scenarios on your expectations about the events that would follow your choice, particularly in terms of the alternative reactions from the other players in the network.

Next, for each option you are considering, look ahead and identify which of these possible endgames are plausible. In a network setting, plausibility tests whether the choices expected of these other players are in equilibrium. For an endgame to be *qualified*, it must be plausible.

Then you must choose the option that yields the most preferred of these plausible endgames. This most preferred option is the target of current strategy.

Clearly, in this sequence, the plausibility test is crucial. The test is also important, because innovators are often tempted to skip ahead to the most preferred option. In a networked world, in which the outcome of an innovator's choices is so interdependent with the choices of other players, ignoring the crucial question of plausibility can result in decisions that essentially miss the intended target. For example, the thirty-thousand-cell, Excel-based model previously described brought into sharp focus the suboptimality of ignoring plausibility. A plausibility check completely inverted the original most preferred decision.

The model case was a simplified example to motivate and illustrate the power of this form of reasoning and its role in making better strategic choices. How does the principle help in making better choices in more general situations, with a wider network of players involved?

Qualifying the endgame is, in essence, a screen for deciding between several strategic alternatives that present themselves to an innovator at the start of the campaign. The screening works in two ways. First, it helps eliminate choices that are bound to miss their intended target. Second, it helps an innovator reconfirm if a current strategic choice meets the conditions necessary for success, given the information available at the outset.

A test for plausibility in a general setting would involve the following steps:

- Specify a set of endgame conditions by describing choices to be expected of the key players in the future outcome.

- Test if these conditions meet the criterion of being in equilibrium. In particular, determine that the players' choices are mutual best choices, given what is currently known or assumed about the choice factors driving each player's choices.

Consider two examples that will be discussed in detail in the following sections. In the first example, a strategic option actually pursued would have been eliminated, had the player worked back from the qualifying conditions. What's more, this screening would have been possible with the data available at the time of the decision; the data was not new information that became apparent in hindsight. In the second example, we consider an innovative software application that did indeed become a widely adopted industry standard. With the benefit of hindsight, we will see that the endgame targeted by the early choices was "qualified." Because it was qualified, the innovation succeeded even though it apparently lacked several essential functionalities that would have argued against its potential for success.

The Difference Between an Oracle and Larry Ellison

There is an old Silicon Valley joke. Question: What's the difference between God and Larry Ellison? Answer: God doesn't think he's Larry Ellison.[2] In ancient times, people looked to oracles, who specialized in qualifying the endgames of crucial campaigns. Pythia of Delphi was frequently on call to forecast the outcome of wars. In the modern business world, corporate visionaries take on the oracle's mantle or, at the very least, have it thrust on them. In this regard, few can match Larry Ellison, CEO of Oracle.

Back in 1997, Ellison had declared war on the all-powerful PC. "I hate the PC," he said, but that was not all.[3] "I believe it's time for a new device—the network computer, or NC." His alternative was a new product with an innovative paradigm for distributing computing resources through a network. The proposition to the buyer was an elementary one: His device would cost less than the PC.

Ellison did have some alternatives for how the idea could be positioned: "Think of it [the NC] as an electronic pencil. It's radically easier to use than existing machines because it has less in it to control." An easier-to-use alternative to the PC was a possible route to market. The NC was, nevertheless, positioned primarily as a lower-cost alternative, explained Ellison: "And because it has less, it costs less . . . less than $500 now, and as little as $200 or $300 within a few years."[4]

Consider the business environment in which PCs were being used at the time. Computing systems in most large corporations had a client/server architecture. The PC was the client. It had several powerful stand-alone applications that it could run independently, but it would also connect to servers for communications, database access, or storage applications. Ellison's NC would be thought of as a "thin" client. With minimal stand-alone capability, it would run all its applications hosted by a "fat" server.

Ellison's company Oracle was joined in this mission by two other powerful players: Sun Microsystems, whose JavaOS (a compact, Java-based operating system) was to be the operating system for running NCs, and IBM, itself an influential champion of Java applications, whose servers would benefit from the additional processing demands placed on it by the NC architecture. Oracle would benefit from increased reliance on its database and software capabilities under this new architecture.

In addition to all these direct benefits, the players would have a common interest in establishing an alternative to the "Wintel" (Microsoft Windows plus Intel) dominance of the industry. Although Ellison's coalition had taken on the formidable task of dismantling a powerful equilibrium built around the PC makers and the Wintel coalition, it had sound economic logic, sound technology, and the collective market relationships of three industry giants (and others such as Netscape and Novell) on its side.[5]

Consider, first, the economic logic, which is usually sufficient for getting many innovations past the gate. Everything about the NC architecture made sense from the perspective of efficient allocation of resources. The status quo had PCs on the desks of individuals who used only a fraction of the computer's processing resources. This redundancy was being repeated from desk to desk, resulting in an inefficient use of resources. The cost of a PC was high not only because of the high onetime cost of purchase, but also because of the large recurring expenditure of maintaining and tracking the software on every employee's unit. Many converging trends — network-based computing applications, the spread of Internet usage, and outsourcing of business processes — were working in favor of a reconsideration of this model.

In contrast, the NC model would minimize the computational power that would reside in the client. Most applications would borrow computational intelligence from a server on an as-needed basis. The hardware on the NC would be simpler and significantly cheaper to produce; much of the software would be centralized and shared among users. A 1997 Gartner Group study even quantified the savings in total cost of ownership, predicting on the order of 39 percent savings to a corporate buyer. Although the exactitude of such numbers was debatable, the basic logic appeared unimpeachable: The PC-based status-quo paradigm was the equivalent of airline companies' sending over a private jet for every trip to Grandma's.

Besides the economics, there were other complementary developments from both the demand side and the supply side of the market. On the demand side, sizable segments were considered potential early adopters. Such users would, for instance, be in corporate back-office departments, such as payroll, finance, and customer care, where PCs were used for routine work on a limited set of applications. Many applications in such departments make use of centralized databases. Because purchasing decisions are centralized in these departments, companies look here for opportunities to reduce costs. Moreover, with centralized purchasing, the user has relatively little say in the decision process.

On the supply side, the long-standing relationships and reputations of companies like Oracle, IBM, and Sun certainly gave the movement credibility and market power. The pioneering work of both Sun and IBM, as well as the growing popularity among independent developers in the evolution of Java operating systems and applications software, was clearly going to help in giving NC users an alternative to the Windows suite from Microsoft.

The logical argument in favor of the NC was such that even the incumbents in the PC status quo were getting prepared for a switch-over. Several PC OEMs had begun to include network computers on their product roadmaps; some were in production. Even Microsoft was backing its own version of Java, called ActiveX, and was ready to support a rival network computer product with similar features, the NetPC. The stage had been set for the next big transformation in computing.

In 2003, about six years since the beginning of the campaign, the PC still ruled, and the fate of the NC—or, for that matter, the NetPC—is unknown. The NC had met and exceeded most criteria required of a credible alternative to the PC, yet the status quo survived. What happened?

For an answer, we must recreate the qualifying conditions for an NC-favorable endgame. We can then test the endgame's plausibility by referring back to the status quo and the choice factors to determine if the affected players could reasonably be expected to switch to the qualifying conditions.

A highly probable early adopter segment being targeted by the NC coalition was the corporate back office. Adoption by this segment would also be consistent with the lower-cost positioning of the NC. Within the context of this segment, let us deconstruct the endgame. Consider four crucial parties:

- **Buyers:** demand-side players who decide to purchase PCs or NCs for the department

- **Users:** demand-side players who work in the department

- **The NC coalition:** supply-side players from Oracle, Sun, and IBM

- **OEMs:** supply-side players who manufacture PCs

The NC's success would require the conditions laid out in table 4-4. Of course, other conditions can be added to this list to fill out the story of an "NC wins" endgame. For the purposes of checking for plausibility, however, it is sufficient to specify the *minimal* set of conditions for the NC's success. The second part of the plausibility test requires deciding if these conditions meet the mutual best-choice criteria, a prerequisite for an equilibrium.

TABLE 4-4

"NC Wins" Endgame: Qualifying Conditions

Demand Side	Supply Side
Buyers: They find the PC–NC price differential a sufficiently compelling proposition to be motivated to switch. The differential must compensate for the direct and indirect costs of making the transitions and upgrades.	*NC coalition:* This group expects that with sufficient scale and cost efficiency, a PC–NC price differential can be maintained in the long term. In the intermediate term, even if the NCs are not profitable, they are worthwhile investments.
Users: Any user resistance to the introduction of NCs or user influence on the buying decision is low.	*PC OEMs:* They are unable or unwilling to reduce PC prices to counter the PC–NC price differential.

Choice Factors for Buyers

Being responsible for buying the equipment used by the employees in various departments, the buyers were motivated by the various applications that the computers would facilitate. The other major motivator, as well as constraint, was the budget outlay necessary to meet the department's needs for computing. Buyers would also be motivated by the need to keep systems service calls under control.

Expectations about the choices of buyers in other units or firms with which this department interacts would also play a role. It is important to maintain compatibility to smoothly communicate or exchange information. The expectations about what others are buying also drives expectations about the software and support that would be available from the providers.

In larger corporations, the computing architecture used a client-server model configured with the PC as the client. Any change in the client device would have required upgrading the capabilities of these other components of the system. This would be a distinct constraint to adopting an alternative to the entrenched status quo; the costs in the existing network and servers were already sunk. Change would require the activation of a new buying process for these other parts of the information technology infrastructure.

Choice Factors for Users

Users are, in general, motivated by the desire to do their job without having to relearn how to use a device or get used to new software or interfaces. They would usually prefer the attributes of the PC over those of the NC since they do not bear the direct costs of purchase. The PC gives them the control and flexibility to utilize a vast amount of computing power independently. With a PC, the user can run programs with minimal reliance on connection to a wider network.

Choice Factors for the NC Coalition

The coalition was motivated by the desire to supplant the PC with the NC. However, for each coalition member, the degree to which it would be willing to invest in selling NCs was constrained by several other factors. The NC applications and operating system had not sufficiently matured. There was insufficient market impetus for their development at optimal scale. With the Internet and e-business initiatives emerging as the single biggest attention-grabber for executives at Oracle, IBM, and Sun, as well as their most demanding customers, the coalition's marketing and sales resources were feeling constrained.

Choice Factors for the PC OEMs

A critical constraint governing the PC OEMs' choices was the PC industry structure. When the NC was being launched, the PC had become more of a commodity, with relatively low entry barriers into the PC manufacturing and assembly business. Among the so-called tier-one OEMs, there was intense competition for the high-end PCs. A similar pattern existed among lower-end PCs as well, which were continuing to take potential customers away from tier one. This dynamic was reinforced by a highly competitive component-manufacturing industry serving the OEMs.

The combination of easy entry into PC assembly, increased competitiveness, and standardization resulted in a diminished potential for product differentiation across different brands of PCs. Much of the motivation among PC OEMs was becoming focused on taking costs out of the system. The OEMs were being pushed further in this direction by the competitiveness among component makers, by the continued streamlining of production and supply-chain processes, and by the simplification of the distribution model.

Putting the Choice Factors Together

This brings us to the final part of the plausibility test. Each of these choice factors for all the players was in place and would be common knowledge before the campaign to bring the NC to market and determine the strategy for its positioning. The qualifying conditions for the NC-wins endgame would also be visible when the NC strategy was being determined (see table 4-4). A comparison of the qualifying conditions with the actual conditions would show—in advance of the NC's eventual fate— that the endgame being targeted was *not* a plausible one. Let us see how the NC's endgame would unravel in light of the choice factors. Note that the conditions are interconnected: If one fails, others would come tumbling down as well.

Consider the PC OEM condition necessary to motivate the NC buyers: the PC–NC price differential. As discussed earlier, the PC industry was highly competitive and tending toward little differentiation among the OEMs. Moreover, with a focus on reducing costs of production and logistics and on simplifying the distribution model, the PC industry was structurally primed for a steady lowering of prices.

As a result, the qualifying condition for the buyers to stay in this hypothetical endgame was turning out to be implausible, as the PC–NC price differential was destined for a path of steady erosion. In fact, soon after the NC's introduction, the sub-$1,000 PC category became one of the industry's fastest-growing segments.

Making the condition even more unattainable was that additional investments were necessary for the NC to be integrated into the existing systems in a corporation. Not all the applications could be seamlessly transferred from PC to NC; some user retraining would be required. Additionally, the NC's Java-based software had not sufficiently matured. If the NC were to function as well as the PC, a company's network and servers also needed to be upgraded. The vendors and customer-care representatives for the other parts of the system were not necessarily coordinated with the NC sales force. In the meantime, from a user perspective, no one department in a corporate organization would have the motivation to push for a switch away from the predominant industry standard. This would have been a risky move, given the justifiable expectation that most other users and departments would not be switching, either.

In sum, the NC's primary point of value had been focused on the notion that it was a less-expensive alternative to the PC. The nature of the choice factors driving the highly competitive PC industry had effectively resulted in a closing of the price gap. The PC industry had de facto neutralized the NC's differential value proposition through its own internal competitiveness across PC brands. Buying behaviors were structurally incapable of changing over to the NC in the way it was positioned. The lower-cost-positioned NC was not on course toward its intended endgame.

The qualification process we just went through after the fact could also have been done before the NC campaign was under way. In this way, the principle of reasoning back from the endgame could have helped eliminate losing strategic options and stimulate the search for more viable, potentially winning, alternatives.

How a Portable Format Avoided Being Deported

Once every few years, we are advised to prepare for the paperless office. Yet paper, it seems, is everywhere. It continues to spew forth from printers, fax machines, and photocopiers and fills our mailboxes in even greater volume than before. The content of this paper is varied and is created by many word-processing, graphics, and image-processing programs, as well as by hand.

The problem with communicating using these different formats is that they would need different software applications to be compatible with various forms of communications systems. This incompatibility would be further exacerbated by the limitations of the users' equipment. Also, although some users might need to modify the content of a document, others may need to protect the content from being modified or reproduced. As a result, creators, reproducers, and those who store content are often compelled to maintain and pass on the content on a physical hard copy every time it gets transported to a "reader."

This was the status quo that John E. Warnock, a cofounder of Adobe Corporation, wanted to resolve with the Adobe Acrobat PDF (portable document format).[6] The idea was to create a uniform standard for reproducing the image of any document without any changes to its visual appearance, and then transmitting it in a form that could be read with a reader-application software conforming to the same standard.

The journey to an endgame for such an application was not without its perils. There were different forms of software and hardware to bring together under this portable format. The forms and origins of the content were disparate. Moreover, any product positioned as the multiplatform standard for sharing images would face strong opposition from the creators of word- or image-processing software, since they would wish to be the standard themselves.

In addition, for the format to become a standard, a critical mass of users would have to adopt it, which would be a daunting task without the kind of leverage that a player such as Microsoft has. Apart from its technical decisions, Adobe made a strategic choice on two important fronts: One was to design a system so that the reader could not make changes to the document. The other decision was to give away part of the program for free and in an easily downloadable form. This meant resisting the temptation to create a more versatile format in which readers could interact with and manipulate the documents they would receive. It also meant forgoing a revenue stream from readers, who would presumably outnumber those who create the content.

In developing a strategy, an innovator would need to consider these four players:

- **Content creators:** demand-side players who need to store and distribute content

- **Content readers:** demand-side players who need easy access to the content

- **Distribution channels:** supply-side players that make the content available

- **Software, applications, and hardware providers:** supply-side players that provide direct and indirect support

The demand-side group includes players on two ends of the content that needs portability: the content creators and readers. The choice factors of both sets vary according to the type of content and its origin. The key supply-side players include those in distribution and those that provide enabling products. In the first category are the various distribution channels, such as Web sites and corporate networks, over which the content is made available, as well as the content readers who refer other readers to the content or pass it along electronically. The second category of players includes the providers of complementary software, applications, and platforms. This category covers not only Microsoft and Apple, whose products are instrumental in the creation and reading of documents, but also those with enabling products, such as search engines and digital imaging software and hardware.

Table 4-5 lays out the qualifying conditions for the Acrobat-favored endgame. Is this configuration a plausible endgame? It clearly is, as the following analysis will show. In fact, the creators of the Adobe Reader and Creator suite used the potential to create such an endgame quite effectively to establish the Adobe Acrobat as the standard for communicating and sharing documents regardless of the methods or even the many varieties of software used to create them.

To check for plausibility, we need to consider if the mutual best-response criteria are met. These can be tested through

TABLE 4-5

Acrobat-Favored Endgame: Qualifying Conditions

Demand Side	Supply Side
Content creators: This group uses the PDF software to store and distribute the content to its desired audience. Content creators are motivated to place content in a form ready for the distribution channels by transferring it to a PDF file. Many should also find value in the assurance that the content cannot be changed or reproduced outside the intended context after distribution.	*Distribution channels:* This group routinely places content reproduced in PDF files on Web sites or in electronic communications. Most of the Web sites that host such content should also make it easy to access the Acrobat reader software—at low cost. This group also includes content readers who pass PDF files to other readers with the expectation that the files will be readable by the recipients.
Content readers: This group derives value from accessing, viewing, and printing—and not needing to modify—the content in a convenient, readable, and cost-effective way. These players would routinely use the Acrobat reader to access the content. They want easy access to such documents and a simple process for acquiring the necessary reader software.	*Software, applications, and hardware providers:* The equipment and software needed to create and download the files should be standard and easily available. Finally, the primary content-creation software (word- and image-processing and communications applications) providers, such as Microsoft, should view the Acrobat reader as a complement to their own products and, as a result, have no motivation to resist its proliferation. Other complementary products, such as scanners, digital cameras, printers, other forms of digital imaging equipment, and software should be experiencing increasing adoption.

the choice factors that govern the behaviors of the players in the endgame.

Choice Factors for Content Creators

Content creators are motivated by the desire to gain exposure to the widest segment of the intended audience for their content. They are also motivated by the need to find the most appropriate and cost-effective channels to distribute the content. Their constraints are defined by the relative difficulty of distributing content to their potentially widespread audience.

These difficulties are compounded when the content has been prepared in a nonstandard format and cannot be shared easily as an electronic file attachment. In particular, many content creators are interested in having the content read in the same form in which it was produced. They also want to protect the original document by ensuring that the reader cannot alter it.

Choice Factors for Content Readers

Content readers are motivated by the need to access content that creates value to them and is relevant for their business, educational, and personal interests. They are interested in accessing the content in a way that reduces the costs of search and transaction. They want to avoid having to sift through information to determine its quality and relevance. Any technology that helps them reach the appropriate content has to be relatively easy to use. The readers' constraints are those of cost, complexity, compatibility with their existing systems, and the other demands on their time and resources.

Content readers are sometimes motivated to access certain documents because they wish to modify them themselves; other times, they wish only to read for informational purposes. Occasionally, this separation is hard to make, but in general, readers are comfortable with this distinction and it fits with their needs.

Choice Factors for the Distribution Channels

The channels are motivated by the growth of their own business or other interests, such as the efficient transmission of information and data in a community. To the extent that some content helps further these interests, and if there is overlap between the audiences, distribution channels would be willing both to host the content and to help in its distribution. For example, a corporate Web site may wish to place publicity brochures and white papers to communicate its point of view on its industry and the value of its product. It may also want to place news items, white papers, and articles by others on the site. The channel wants to place the content in the format that assures wide readership. The distribution channel's constraints are given by the nature of the content it considers to be in its interests, the resources used, and the other costs of carrying the content.

Choice Factors for the Enabling Software, Applications, and Hardware Providers

The motivators and constraints for these players are similar to those for the distribution channels. The providers' primary interest is in promoting greater usage of their products. To the extent that none of them has a product directly threatened by PDF, they would be motivated to promote its usage since greater transfer of digital and other files increases the use of other products in the system. Players that have word-, graphics-, and image-processing software of their own would be supportive of PDF, assuming that it is not used to produce original documents. This way, the PDF would not compete with their products and would act instead as a complement to them.

Putting the Choice Factors Together

Juxtaposing the qualifying conditions with the choice factors yields an internally consistent picture. Each critical player is making a best choice, given the expectations about the corresponding best choices being made by the others. The endgame passes the test of equilibrium and qualifies as plausible. It is, of course, also an endgame that favors wide adoption of the Adobe Acrobat suite. With more than 300 million downloads of the Acrobat reader by 2002, the application has apparently capitalized on the opportunity. Acrobat is the de facto standard for downloading documents with their original appearance over the Web or in other electronic communications.

Adobe Acrobat's success may be considered somewhat surprising if we were to turn the clock back to the early 1990s. Then, the innovation was being launched into a world dominated by tools such as the universally used Microsoft Office at one end and specialized graphic-design software at the other. The Adobe Acrobat was a counterintuitive entry into an environment in which the users were accustomed to interacting and modifying any document they could access electronically. Having stuck to its noninteractive feature, Adobe created a market for itself with a consistent endgame. It did so by simultaneously serving the crucial needs of other players while avoiding the triggering of defensive action from established software companies whose products were used to create original content. The players' interconnection with each other validates the initial strategic choices made by Adobe.

FOUR BROAD ISSUES FOR PLANNING STRATEGY

In sum, the principle of endgame reasoning is an approach to using the future as a way to screen various strategic options available to the innovator in the present. These options determine the broad direction that the path to market will take. They could include major decisions such as competitive positioning, product features and benefits, technology choice, and pricing. Although a principle of employing the future to guide current choice might seem intuitive, we have seen in practice that the application of the concept can be hard. Precisely for this reason, it is crucial for endgame reasoning to be hard-wired into the way an innovator's organization plans strategy.

Translating endgame reasoning into an organization's planning process requires keeping track of four issues.

From Multiple Scenarios to Focused Endgames

Strategies prepared for inherently uncertain market conditions frequently lead planners to develop several market scenarios. Scenario analysis is a way to prepare for multiplicity. Instead of fixing a single set of assumptions on which to consider choices, scenario analysis offers a framework to do so with variations on the assumptions. In this way, an innovator can gauge both upside and downside consequences.[7]

When your objective is to take an innovation to market, you should keep in mind several aspects of the process. First, a classic benefit of working through many scenarios is that it can steer planners toward choices that can do well in multiple circumstances. Because innovations typically call for greater risk taking, planners may need to make trade-offs and focus aggressively on specific scenarios.

Second, like Escher's *Drawing Hands*, the strategist's actions and the novel aspects of the innovation can profoundly affect the likelihood of the different scenarios. For example, Amazon.com's collaborative filtering software gave users the opportunity to discover books in the "neighborhood" of what they had originally set out to search for. The result was a two-way relationship between the visitor and Web site. Both provide input to the other; the Web site is not simply a passive point of purchase for the visitor. Because of this interconnectivity, a planner needs to take a more active position on the scenarios. They should not be treated as a fixed range of uncertain outcomes set by outside forces.

Third, given the networked nature of the market, a significant source of uncertainty lies in the dynamics of move and countermove among the interconnected players. An aggregated view in terms of a scenario may miss some key insights related to tracing the origins of such uncertain outcomes and the roles played by individual motivations and constraints.

For this reason, I have supplanted the classic projection of alternate scenarios with the more dynamic notion of an endgame. The planner must begin with the endgames that are possible, which is the hallmark of scenario analysis, and then go further to narrow the range. This also makes scenario thinking actionable by asking what behavior must be orchestrated for each player en route to the endgame.

Planning for Contingencies and Early Warning Signals

Endgame reasoning is not meant as a crystal ball for the future. It is a way to target and act on the future using the data and assumptions currently at your disposal. At the same time, you should remain open to the possibility that the target may have to be revised as new information emerges, or as a less preferred yet plausible endgame might be realized. Some forethought about what these alternatives might be, under what circumstances they might arise, and what the earliest warning signal might be—all these constitute the process of the contingency planning.

The more contingencies in your planning assumptions, the more flexibility you would want to retain in the form of commitments you make early on. Of course, this thinking must be accompanied by good judgment. The campaign plan cannot be so weighed down by alternative contingencies, early warning systems, and points of flexibility that all action becomes weighed down by the complexity. Nevertheless, this raises the question of the degree of commitment to the initial strategic choice. Is it firm, or can it be reversed? Are there backup plans in parallel that offer protection from any downside risk? I return to this point in chapter 7.

Using Market Segmentation to Qualify the Endgame

A market can typically be partitioned into several distinct segments. In introducing an innovation, an innovator normally first considers a segment of a market in which adoption is most likely, as we did in the case of the NC. If the addressable market were considered in its entirety, several endgames could fail the plausibility test. When they fail in the most likely segments, as happened with the NC, we know that the strategic choice under consideration will not succeed. When this happens, we can consider either alternative strategic options, alternative segments of the market, or even subsegments to target, provided they are worth the pursuit in the first place.

One of the more dramatic illustrations of the transformation of a potentially unqualified endgame into a highly qualified one simply by choosing the right market segment comes from the world of pharmaceuticals. SmithKline Beecham had introduced Paxil, a third entrant in a new breakthrough class of antidepressants, the SSRIs (selective serotonin re-uptake inhibitors). Two blockbusters—Prozac, the leader from Eli Lilly, and Zoloft, the second-mover from Pfizer—already occupied the market. Paxil had little chance of achieving blockbuster status (or approximately $1 billion-plus in annual sales) with clinical data not very different from those of the incumbents. An endgame in which the three would occupy roughly a third of the market seemed unattainable in an undifferentiated, unsegmented market; neither incumbent seemed likely to budge to accommodate a new entrant in any conceivable scenario.

It turned out, though, that Paxil did have a sedative side effect in its clinical profile. SmithKline Beecham decided to use that information to segment the market into depressed patients who also display anxiety, for whom Paxil's sedative impact would be beneficial. The strategy worked. Paxil's positioning on anxiety was reinforced by Prozac's position of being ideal for melancholic patients, thereby giving Paxil rights to an alternative segment. Zoloft took on the segments that displayed both anxiety and melancholia or neither. A new, mutually reinforcing endgame had been found with three blockbuster products in the same market, each playing to a different segment.[8]

Being Disciplined About Reasoning Backward

Endgame reasoning may appear quite reasonable in principle, especially given the benefits we have observed in the preceding examples. With its logic running counterclockwise or backward in time, it is difficult to practice consistently. As the number of players on the critical path increases or the specifics of the market situation become more complicated or the sequence of play lengthens, the backward logic can become quite difficult to sustain. Yet, it is essential for good strategic choice. This reasoning skill can be acquired with repeated exposure to the same or similar strategic situations.

Endgame reasoning adds value in situations in which the choices of others affects our own choices; without this form of reasoning, we may make less than optimal choices. It becomes hardwired into our thinking for routine decisions, for example, playing familiar sports, driving home during rush hour, competing in a market in which we have played many times before, and even getting to the airport on time.

To get to the airport on time you automatically reason backward from your previous experiences. You estimate how much time it will take to check in and to go through the security checkpoints, not just for yourself, but for everyone else flying. All this adds to the time it takes to board a flight. Where you park your vehicle will also add a certain amount of time to the process. So will the traffic you expect on the way to the airport. You fine-tune the time estimate based on what you know about the time of day, the day of the week, the proximity to peak air travel times, and other conditions that affect how everybody else will be making choices. You create a scenario of how busy and complicated the airport ticketing and security screening will be; then you add all these factors into your decision for what you do before going to the airport. If you expect the security to be tighter or the traffic to be heavier, for instance, you may plan to leave your home or office earlier. Or, to free up some extra time needed at the end, you may finish an appointment earlier than you otherwise would. What you are doing here is simply beginning with a set of endgame conditions for making it to the destination on time and then working backward from them to test if they are consistent with the factors that govern the choices en route.

Less-experienced travelers tend to over- or underbudget the amount of time they will need to get through the "airport endgame." Without experience, a person cannot easily imagine the future first before making choices in the present. The airport example is an illustration of endgame reasoning in our day-to-day affairs. But we resist practicing the discipline when confronted with significantly new and unique strategic challenges. We automatically tend to make choices based on a unilateral projection of what is known today, without considering the alternative reactions that could follow. This tendency is similar to the inclination to pick the seemingly dominant choice in the thirty-thousand-cell model.[9]

Consistent endgame reasoning has an additional advantage: It may offer a source of asymmetric competitive advantage. If you are systematically more disciplined in following this line of reasoning, you are already ahead of the game relative to your competitors.

MAINTAINING a backward-reasoning discipline means beginning with a guess about the end, which often runs against our natural inclinations. It is even harder when the environment from which we must reason back is a network of many connected choices. Innovators—risk takers with strong convictions by nature—would be tempted to take the Napoleonic counsel *On s'engage et puit on voit!* ("Jump in the fray and find out what happens!"). The danger with jumping into a network whose behavior you do not quite understand in the aggregate is that it could take off in one of many different directions. You could be left with a strategic choice that is a mismatch for the direction the market takes once the network has responded to your initiative. Therefore, it is wise to consider first the fray that will follow so that you know which fray is worthwhile jumping—or even sticking a toe—into.

Chapter Five

TUNNELING TO THE VISION

The future is not invented; it is co-evolved
with a wide class of players.

—John Seely Brown, chief scientist,
Xerox and former director, Xerox PARC

WITH YET ANOTHER ROUND of escalation of the crisis in the Middle East, both President George W. Bush and Crown Prince Abdullah of Saudi Arabia offered another set of possible visions for the future of the region, which prompted an interesting comment from the Israeli foreign minister Shimon Peres. Both visions, he noted, were like "lights at the end of a tunnel—but with no tunnel."[1] As we sadly have come to know, without the tunnel, what lies at the end of it does little good. Establishing a vision and qualifying it is a necessary first step for ushering in any new idea. You need to build the tunnel to get you there.

The challenge doubles when you consider the gravitational attraction of the status quo. A mechanism is needed not only to coordinate the choices of a network of players to conform with the endgame conditions; it also must provide the ballast necessary to break out of the status quo's orbit. As the discussion of the health-care system in chapter 1 makes clear, breaking out is not easy.

Consider the breakout plans of innovation maven Jim Clark, whose earlier successes included the launch of Netscape. His campaign to find a solution to the informationally inefficient state of the health-care sector led to the creation of Healtheon, which later became WebMD.

The timing of Healtheon's entry was propitious. The Internet was creating an opportunity for the various players on the health-care network to connect over a common platform without high up-front investment and on an affordable subscription basis. This low-cost and easy-to-use facility could be critical to getting physicians, the pivotal players, to sign up and so bring the rest of the system along.

Healtheon/WebMD's strategy was to be the common platform, with links to physicians and all other crucial parties in health care. The strategy was based on an understanding of the various choice factors driving physicians to select a preferred method of connecting with others. Thus, creating simple, easy-to-use linkages with a sound, underlying business logic would be part of the minimal conditions for a successful endgame. With this objective in mind, Healtheon/WebMD's founders systematically set about acquiring or partnering with supply-side players that could help provide the needed motivation to all key parties in the health-care network. The founders' goal was to form an integrated platform.

Table 5-1 outlines Healtheon/WebMD's moves from February 1999 to February 2000 to match a demand-side endgame condition with a supply-side player. If the firm could coordinate all these players to create an integrated platform for a physician's information needs, a critical mass of users would be motivated to sign up. In effect, Healtheon/WebMD would have orchestrated both the supply side and the demand side of a new equilibrium.

TABLE 5-1

Healtheon/WebMD's Mechanisms to Configure an Endgame

Demand-Side Service Area	Healtheon/WebMD's Moves to Coordinate Supply-Side Solution
Patient content and commerce	Acquires WebMD, OnHealth Network
	Partners or forms marketing alliance with HealthSouth, CVS.com, Yahoo!, Reader's Digest, Lycos, and CNN
Patient-physician content	Acquires WebMD
	Partners and allies with Medtronic and News Corporation
Physician content and practice management	Acquires WebMD, Medical Manager, CareInsite, Medcast Networks
	Invests in Vitalworks.com
Physician-institution connectivity	Acquires Envoy, Kinetra, MEDE America
Health-care provider and payer automation	Partners with Coventry Health, TriWest, Humana, Arup Laboratories, HealthSouth

Source: Data compiled from Healtheon/WebMD annual report, 2000.

And yet, despite the multisided approach to this multisided problem, Healtheon/WebMD failed to bring about fast change. Its acquisition of Medical Manager topped a *Business Week* list of the worst mergers.[2] In hindsight, we can see many reasons for why this ambitious strategy failed. The beginning of the collapse of Internet-centered businesses in general and the loss of confidence by the capital markets in the spring of 2000 eroded the firm's credibility and resources. Most important, Healtheon/WebMD had made a crucial error: It had correctly taken a networked view of the changes it would need to coordinate, but in doing so it spread its resources over too many points of attack. Adding to the bind was that it had seriously overpaid for several acquisitions. The organizational and resource challenges of integrating so many different entities and capabilities and of managing a multilateral customer front were overwhelming.

What was the lesson? An innovator must focus its resources on select points of leverage. Ideally, these points should have multiplier effects throughout the rest of the system. This means taking advantage of the network's connectivity and exerting influence on some players, who then propagate the influence to others. These methods for spreading influence are called *multiplier mechanisms*. The trick, of course, is to ensure that you are approaching the right players to get the innovation to spread to a point of critical mass.

This chapter discusses the different ways of orchestrating such multiplier mechanisms. Creating such a mechanism is the second aspect of the campaign to get innovation into market.

WHY GENERAL MULTIPLIER EFFECTS ARE IMPORTANT

The status quo has a crucial advantage. It is already in equilibrium. The purpose of innovation is to act as a disequilibrating force. An innovation, of course, may often be a better product or a unique solution to an existing inefficiency, but it has no special powers to successfully untangle an equilibrium's entrenched status quo. We already know, for example, that there are economic advantages to networks that have superior scale. The status quo, by definition, looms over any proposed innovation, since it has a ready-made network associated with it.

How do you, from this asymmetric start, build up to an endgame in which the gravitational pull flips over to a competing outcome anchored around your innovation? The Healtheon/WebMD illustration alerts us to the risks posed by spreading resources too widely across the network. As suggested, the answer may lie in focusing efforts on parts of the system that act as multiplier mechanisms.

THE HUB MECHANISM

There is no uniform formula for finding the right places to intervene in a networked market. No magical step can guarantee that its own effects will multiply and encourage the adoption of an innovation. Many factors, including an innovation's characteristics, its differences from the status-quo product or service, and the characteristics of the market involved, help determine what approach will work best.

An intuitive place to begin is by finding the *hubs* of the network, in other words, the players that connect to many others. Malcolm Gladwell of the *New Yorker* has a simple experiment for finding hubs in a social network.[3] He gives you a list of 250 randomly drawn last names from the Manhattan phone book and asks if you know anybody by that name. Scores are assigned for every name you associate with an acquaintance. Gladwell ran the experiment with diverse groups of people. There were extraordinarily high scorers in every social group he tested. His conclusion? In every walk of life, some people have a "truly extraordinary knack of making friends and acquaintances."

Most of us know people like that and often turn to them to spread influence to a wider group. (Theodore Roosevelt, as an extreme example, had more than twenty-two thousand acquaintances.[4]) In a market, even a highly fragmented one, it is similarly easy to identify hublike players. A natural place to begin in thinking about multiplier mechanisms is to organize around such a hub. In fact, the ideal position may well be to become one.

Hubs, in our context, are the players and products that interconnect with a broad set of additional players on the critical path to an endgame. In addition to—and, frequently, because of—connecting with so many players, hubs wield considerable influence. In particular, hubs have the opportunity to modify various choice factors that govern the choices of other players because of their direct access and leverage. Given the resources and scale advantages necessary to assemble a hub, there are usually only a few hubs in a network, but that small number can give access to a critical mass across the entire network.

Some familiar names—for good reason—come to mind when we think of hubs in different industries: the local phone companies in telecommunications, Microsoft in software and computer applications, eBay in Internet commerce, Cisco in data networking, and AOL Time Warner in media and Internet services. If an innovation were originated by a hub, it would enjoy an instant distribution network and the leverage to encourage wide adoption.

In retrospect, we can reverse-engineer the sequence by which successful hubs, some intentionally and others by accident, became powerful as a multiplier mechanism. For example, eBay certainly was not—as is widely believed—the first mover in Internet commerce to use auctions as the means to buy and sell. It did, however, make several good decisions, which has resulted in its hublike status. What started out as a site for founder Pierre Omidyar's girlfriend to share her Pez candy dispensers with others who were similarly inclined has played host to kidneys, rare art, and a Miami high-schooler's virginity, not to mention IBM computers, antique china, and time-shares. With more than 2 million auctions and 250,000 new items listed on any given day, eBay is often referred to as the most successful Internet commerce venture. It accounted for about 20 percent of all Internet commerce in 2001.[5] More remarkable in the light of the fleeting nature of many of its contemporaries, the company was even profitable.

The success of eBay derives from a combination of elements. Auctions, for one, benefit from the network effect. Having more participants—both buyers and sellers—on a particular auction site attracts even more participants. The sellers expect better pricing for their products and better information to emerge during the bidding process; the buyers expect more sellers and, therefore, more variety and better deals. Buyers also find that having more buyers provides them with information during the bidding against others and makes the process fun. For eBay, this meant that the company had to build up to a critical mass of loyalists, who would then create their own momentum, acting as a multiplier mechanism.

En route, eBay made several smart choices to get to critical mass. For example, its auction rules are designed to minimize the uncertainties that surround an auction and potentially depress the values at which goods sell. Its feedback process helps foster a community feeling and loyalty among users. The users can also rate each other, which further contributes to reducing uncertainty. The company maintains a common platform that is welcoming to individuals, small businesses, and corporate players such as Disney and The Home Depot. With its wide base of buyers and sellers, eBay has dispersed the costs of maintaining an inventory, marketing, shipping, and even customer service. Every piece of its value proposition to an individual user keeps the user loyal to eBay, which reinforces other users to remain loyal to it as well. The company benefits from being at the center of a stable equilibrium.

As mentioned earlier, these choices have turned eBay into a successful hub. If, on the other hand, an innovation is starting from scratch, a position eBay itself was in just a few years ago, how does it get to a hublike status?

In practice, the mechanism for "becoming the next eBay" is expensive and quite risky. Of course, there are success stories, which provide an ongoing source of inspiration. Many more cautionary tales, however, would suggest that the aspiration to create such a mechanism should naturally be approached appropriately, with appropriate caution.

FairMarket Network, a leading provider of software to Internet auction sites, offers a case study in contrast to eBay's. FairMarket's solution was to create an alternative network comprising those players who were similarly locked out of the Internet auctions industry. It was already in the business of setting up and running auctions for others such as Lycos, Dell Auctions, and CompUSA. In September 1999, it created the FairMarket Network, which would include, in addition to the aforementioned players, MSN, Excite@Home, Ticketmaster Online, and more than one hundred other auction sites.

Here is how the plan would work. A seller would list an item through, say, Lycos. This information would be posted on the Web pages of all the other players that had joined the FairMarket Network. A potential buyer at one of these sites would have no idea that the item is listed on Lycos. When another buyer at a different site joins the fray, an auction begins, with FairMarket as the intermediary between the various sites to ensure that the bidding proceeds seamlessly as if the various participants were part of the same network. Adoption for the users was quite simple: They could log into an auction from any participating site.

It seemed for a while that FairMarket had indeed succeeded, at least in raising the hopes of its investors. Its stock rose to fifty dollars per share after the announcement of the network. Over the next several months, however, along with the collapse of the Internet economy, FairMarket's fortunes declined. Its network's revenues did not take off, and its stock price fell to less than two dollars per share. eBay did, after all, enjoy a 90 percent market share and was not part of the Fair-Market Network. Finally, FairMarket made a compromise that, ironically, led back to the original hub. In February 2001, it integrated its services into eBay's site. Businesses that allowed FairMarket's back-end system to hook into their back offices could list items on eBay.

There is certainly conceptual appeal in creating a hub. But it is an approach fraught with risk and can be prohibitively expensive. Sometimes it is just not feasible. Moreover, if a market already has a hub, it is hard to establish an alternative one.

Instead of aiming to become the player with the leverage across the necessary network, it is usually worthwhile exploring alternatives that rely instead on finding points of leverage with other players that already enjoy access to the network.

THE INFECTING MECHANISM

Different multiplier mechanisms have different implications for the extent of direct intervention they require. The hub alternative defines the extreme end of intervention intensity. The more brand-new the network, the more intervention it requires.

At the other extreme are approaches that piggyback on an existing network as the medium through which the innovator can propagate the innovation. One such approach is the infecting mechanism. This approach is appropriate for a situation in which an innovation is directly in competition with the status quo and, simultaneously, the innovator has only limited direct access to the players in the existing network. Consequently, the intervention can happen only at select points in the system.

The mechanism would work as follows. Despite an endgame objective to displace the status quo, the innovation's introduction is designed to be anything but disruptive. The introduction happens in a low-key manner, which piggybacks on the connectivity of the existing market players as the prime channel for spreading multiplier effects.

The introduction is focused on a narrow, early adopter segment. This segment finds the innovation extremely compelling, perhaps because the innovation requires little or no change in behavior. Also, the entry is both targeted and subtle; it flies under the radar. In other words, given the highly focused and subtle manner of introduction, the entry does not trigger a competitive reaction that might nip its growth in the bud.

The second step is the actual process of multiplication. An innovator attempts to multiply its influence by affecting the choice factors governing adoption behavior in segments similar to those already penetrated. Once these secondary segments have been penetrated, a similar path takes it to the segment adjacent to these, and so on, until the innovator has covered a significant portion of the market. This mechanism fully leverages the interconnected nature of a networked market to reach the choice factors of a wider set of players. Each adopter of the innovation becomes a channel to multiple potential adopters. Since every player interacts with several others and succeeds in influencing at least some factors, there is potential for an exponential multiplication of the innovation's adopter base.

Hotmail, Its Successors, and the Infecting Mechanism

The mechanism just described is similar to the notion of viral marketing that gained popularity as marketers were discovering the capabilities of the electronic network.[6] How the irresistible granddaddy of viral marketing examples used this mechanism is worth some attention. In 1996, Sabeer Bhatia and Jack Smith launched a company called Hotmail to offer free e-mail service. It was around the same time as the launch of Juno Online Services, a competitor. Hotmail's advertising budget was a mere $50,000, which paled when compared with Juno's $20 million. Hotmail's initial growth from zero to 12 million users in eighteen months was, arguably, one of the fastest in the history of media companies. Hotmail was acquired by MSN and became the most popular e-mail service, with one in four users of the Web as a customer.

Of course, many factors help explain Hotmail's precedent-setting performance. The service was free. It was launched at one of the steepest points on the growth curve of the single most popular application on the Web: e-mail. Setting up an account was very easy, which appealed to the bulk of its adopters, who were new to the concept of e-mail. In other words, the combination of exponentially growing demand and a zero price made it an unbeatable formula for adoption. As we now know, however, the formula is no guarantee of success. The succeeding years witnessed hundreds of Web-based businesses betting on a similar formula that failed to win adoption despite some early promise.

Although the popularity of free and easy-to-use e-mail was a clear contributor to Hotmail's success, we might wonder how Hotmail's adoption multiplied through the system, especially with a nonexistent marketing campaign. The secret of the diffusion campaign was a highly successful application of an infecting mechanism. Every time a Hotmail e-mail user sent a message to someone else, the message included a promotion and a clickable URL (uniform resource locator) that read: "Get your private free e-mail from (MSN) Hotmail at http://www.Hotmail.com." The recipient's motivation to try this service was heightened by the reminder—often from a trusted correspondent—and instant availability. The ease of establishing an account by clicking on the URL and following simple instructions eliminated several constraints, especially the discomfort of trying something new.

This so-called viral approach was applied in other creative ways as well. The movie *The Blair Witch Project* involved e-mails that gave life to a false rumor about the circumstances under which the movie was shot. Rumors invite propagation. This led to people's passing the word along to their friends and correspondents; in turn, everybody in the chain had to watch the movie to check out if the rumors were true.

The campaign by Electric Artists to market the then relatively unknown pop artist Christina Aguilera also used the viral approach. The company studied teen Web sites, created its own site, posted its own fan messages, and encouraged others to request Aguilera's single "Genie" on the radio and MTV. This action encouraged the formation of an even wider network, making her a sensation before her debut album had appeared.

Benefits of the Electronic Medium in Viral Marketing

The success of viral marketing campaigns such as that of Hotmail has brought into sharp focus several aspects of the electronic medium that facilitate propagation. These aspects can be split into three categories: the architecture, the technology, and the business model that directly addresses the motivators and the constraints of the players affected.

The architecture of electronic networks creates a geometric progression of linkages as one follows the thread of connectivity from player to player. Each player in the network connects to many others, and this multiplies at each successive layer of links. The initial adopters act as channels to a wider group of future adopters.

In addition, several technology-enabled advantages make the electronic network particularly compelling as a medium for the infecting mechanism. Information about any innovation can be distributed easily over the network with an accompanying URL. Since the URLs are hot links (links easily accessed by a click of the mouse) the links in turn lead to a relatively easy access to detailed information about the characteristics, the online purchase, and perhaps the online delivery of the product.

The final electronic advantage to viral marketing, the business model, sets up the right incentives for continued influence on the choice factors that encourage adoption. On the one hand, using an adopter as a channel to the next line of adopters is a relatively low-cost approach to marketing and distribution. On the other hand, the adopter must be motivated to act as a channel.

The most appealing aspect of Hotmail's strategy, of course, was that the motivation was automatic. The e-mail customer had no choice; Hotmail's URL was automatically attached to the messages they were sending to others. In many other instances, a real incentive may be necessary. Such added motivators could range from the psychological (e.g., the desire to share information, as in the case of *The Blair Witch Project*) to financial. The electronic medium has excelled in developing a variety of such motivation schemes; it can systematically keep track of every transaction, thereby creating the data essential for such schemes to work.

A particularly ingenious motivator was the one used by PayPal, a pioneer in online payment services. In two years, the company's reach had extended to 12 million users by early 2002, when at the very least it had won the distinction of becoming the only Internet IPO in almost a year. On PayPal, registered users can send a payment to anyone with an e-mail address by entering the amount online. The recipient fills out a simple form to collect the payment and is instantly registered as a PayPal user as well.

Infecting Mechanisms Beyond Viral Marketing

Although the term *viral marketing* may have originated with the electronic network and with the work of Jeffrey Rayport, my colleague in Monitor's Marketspace, or with Steve Jurvetson, a founding investor in Hotmail, the idea of an infecting mechanism has long predated the Internet. From Tupperware to cosmetics to long-distance phone services, such multilevel marketing campaigns have had a long and sometimes checkered history.

Infecting mechanisms live on beyond the Internet as well in the form of the "buzz" marketing (where consumers spread the word about an innovation to other consumers either through communications or by their actions) used to sell Christina Aguilera's music. Physical products as varied as Ford subcompact cars, Vespa scooters, jeans, and other consumer products have been diffused through the market through such a mechanism.[7] Movies, books, toys, fashion trends, and even pharmaceuticals have always relied on buzz marketing, even if, historically, the mechanism was not as deliberately applied as it is now. In capturing the power of a successful application of the infecting mechanism, Peter Thiel of PayPal put his finger on it: "It's easier than catching a cold."[8]

THE COMPLEMENTING MECHANISM

Innovations are frequently thought of as substitutes for products or processes that exist in the status quo. Claims like "works better," "new and improved," "faster," "more powerful," and even "breakthrough" are common marketing messages that herald the arrival of an innovation. In contrast to these competitive conventions, another approach applies to innovations that can be positioned as a complement to—and not a substitute for—the status-quo products or services. A complementing mechanism is appropriate for an innovator with limited ability to launch a coordinated attack on multiple points in the network. However, this mechanism holds a somewhat wider potential for access than the infecting mechanism.

This alternative has several appealing aspects. First, it builds on the motivators that perpetuate choices around the status quo by creating added benefits within the existing network. Second, it establishes the stand-alone value of the innovation by further validating the status quo rather than disrupting it. Third, through its complementary position, it wards off a strong competitive reaction from incumbents. In other words, it offers the innovator a way to enter and diffuse into a market without having the network effects of the current system work against the innovation. Over time, however, and with a wide enough base of adopters, the innovation can claim a loyal following of its own. With a critical mass, it will have leverage to steer toward a desired endgame—even if the innovation ultimately becomes a substitute for what existed in the status quo.

The Palm Pilot and the Complementing Mechanism

About the same time that Larry Ellison was engaged in getting the NC onto his customers' desks, their hands were reaching instead for a sleek, new device in their pockets: the Palm Pilot.[9] This product was to make new-product-launch history. Definitely not a PC, the Palm Pilot was closer to Ellison's envisioned electronic pencil. Unlike the NC, the new device even had an electronic pencil. The Palm Pilot had risen from the ashes of the Sony Magic Link and the Apple Newton to sell a million units in its first eighteen months.

The Palm literally created a new product category for personal digital assistants (PDAs). Sales of such devices are expected one day to outstrip those of the PC. The Palm has more than ten thousand applications developed by third-party developers, making it the leading operating system in mobile computing. As mobile users become one of the fastest-growing segments of computer and Internet applications customers, the Palm — both the product itself and the software — is positioned to be a major player.

The early attractiveness of the Palm was that it was easy to use. It performed simple, but essential functions and was designed as a scheduling and note-keeping complement to the PC, the information device predominant in the status quo. Increasingly, newer generations of the Palm also include the most important computing and communications functions, such as Internet access, e-mail, and messaging. In addition, users of cell phones or other devices with a Palm-compatible modem can have the same functionality using Palm software.

As it broadens its range of applications and as competing handheld devices gain share and prices come down, Palm will try to steer away from its dependence on the hardware side of its business. Ultimately, Palm's intent is to become the dominant operating system and the de facto standard for mobile applications, much like the position of Microsoft in the traditional PC space.

This raises a crucial question. The Palm had been introduced initially as a complement to the PC. Going forward, is it becoming a competitor to the PC and the equilibrium around it? Many applications that would be performed on the PC have migrated and, increasingly, will migrate to a Palm-like device and use Palm-like software. As Oracle learned with its attempts to introduce the NC, the PC status quo was not an easy one to challenge. How did the Palm get to this point?

Of course, the Palm's very simplicity in form and function, together with savvy marketing, had a lot to do with its success. The Palm's most compelling feature, however, may have been that it involved no disruption of the PC equilibrium. It was a perfect complement to the PC. At its point of entry, it did not displace any of the PC's applications. To the contrary, its synchronization function helped leverage the PC as a server with the Palm as the client. As such, the Palm Pilot was a prototype of a true network computer, albeit with very limited functionality.

The Palm had implemented a complementing mechanism, almost by the book. The product added value to the existing network with minimal change in user behavior. In addition to motivating PC users to seek new applications for the PC, the Palm even helped with some individuals' reluctance to use the PC for purposes such as scheduling and note taking. While helping validate the status quo, it still gained recognition as an innovation that users had fallen in love with. Even the PC OEMs welcomed its arrival. Several manufacturers developed competing products of their own, thereby widening the category. What's more, Microsoft, which was trying to position its Windows CE operating system against the Palm operating system, did little to thwart its progress.

Although the Palm's early applications were stand-alone functions such as scheduling and taking notes, it quickly

accommodated applications that allowed communication between Palm users. Soon the Palm operating system itself could
be used on other wireless devices and could be used to access
the Web. Once the critical mass had been reached, the ground
had been prepared for a new network. Software vendors and
Web sites were motivated to customize their applications and
information to be Palm readable. No matter how much PC
space the Palm eventually gets to occupy in the longer run,
this handheld device has changed the status quo. A new equilibrium, with mobile computing independent of the PC, has
become a reality.

THE COORDINATED INCENTIVES MECHANISM

The mechanisms described thus far are initiated through focused entry into a market. They then rely on a multiplier to get
the innovation into the rest of the network. This multiplier effect is created by leveraging the inherent connectivity of the
status-quo network—in one case, using each link as a channel;
in the other, providing a complementary product. Now, suppose neither approach is available.

An alternative way into the market is to bring about a multiplier effect by assembling an alternative network. To accom-
plish this, an innovator devises a business model—that is, a
value-sharing scheme—that helps coordinate the incentives of
players in three interlinking categories: those who enable and
add to the benefits of the innovation, those who can distribute
it to users, and those who actually benefit by adopting it. The
first two categories of players are on the supply side of the
network to be created; the last is on the demand side. The purpose, of course, is to synchronize the choices of these critical
players in a mutually reinforcing way.

One way to orchestrate such choices is to understand how
the choice of each group affects the others. For example, the
actions of one could be a constraint on those of another.

Changing that set of actions might remove the constraints and create new motivators that get others to change as well. Tracing these linkages offers a guide for a beneficial alignment of incentives. The question is how to make adoption of the innovation a common interest, which gives rise to a virtuous cycle so that each generation of adopters further motivates the choices of others.

This three-way coordination of incentives may well be difficult to achieve. Perhaps it is overly expensive, or perhaps an innovator does not have access to or leverage with the parties. An identification of such gaps would reveal where the innovator may need to extend its reach and leverage through partnerships or even through acquisitions.

Adobe Acrobat and the Coordinated Incentives Mechanism

In chapter 4, we explored the endgame being targeted by Adobe and its portable document format, or PDF. Although the format has been around since the early 1990s, in the founder John Warnock's words, "it has taken a long time to catch on." By 2002, more than 5 million Adobe creator programs had been sold, and more than 300 million readers downloaded. Adobe Acrobat had effectively become electronic paper, electronic photo album, and electronic fax rolled into one.[10]

The path to this outcome involved a delicate balancing of three critical groups: the players who added to the benefits of the PDF, the players who were well positioned to distribute it to adopters, and the adopters themselves. Adobe played an active role in aligning incentives around this triangle in a mutually reinforcing way.

Consider the key choice factors of the first category: specifically, third-party software developers and organizations whose businesses involve developing products around PDF. This group is highly motivated to create new software applications and to share their discoveries with others. A key constraint is their access to the source code of existing software programs, which, if the software developers had it, would allow them to experiment and build on top of it.

Adobe made its code available to developers early on, thereby motivating them to write applications and enhance the features and functionality of the Acrobat product. Over the years, this initiative has generated more than 550 PDF-related tools and products from a wide universe of developers. By 1994, the company had also decided to distribute its reader program for free to users, in an easily downloadable form. As discussed in chapter 4, the company shrewdly decided to offer a free, easily downloaded reader to any user who wanted it.

In the meantime, the feature-rich and easy-to-use tools and related creator products of the Acrobat, particularly the version 4.0, would be highly motivating to those who create content. In addition, the free, easy access to the reader made it attractive to the content creators to store their content in PDF files. In time, the wide variety of content increased the benefit to readers, and, by implication, to the creators of the content.

Acceptance of Acrobat by both sides of the content equation made the product attractive to businesses and Web sites interested in hosting content. These distribution channels also benefited from transferring some content in its original, unalterable form (e.g., application forms, technical drawings, brochures, corporate graphics and colors, and legal documents) to readers, with the expectation that no matter what kind of a system the readers had, they would be able to read the content. Organizations that needed to transfer large documents as well as paper-based documentation (receipts, handwritten notes, drawings, etc.) found it attractive for the same reasons to use the PDF file as a uniform platform for sending and storing information. All of this was made easier by the improved usability of the product suite.

Taking this systemic approach to addressing the interlinked choice factors of three critical groups in the network gave

Adobe a multiplier mechanism that set in motion a virtuous cycle. Increasing use by one party encouraged increased use by the remaining two groups, eliminating many of their constraints and adding to their motivations to become part of the PDF endgame. The catalyst was Adobe's coordinated approach to aligning incentives of those who were key to the adoption process and thereby setting off a multiplier mechanism.

HOW TO TELL WHICH MECHANISM IS MOST APPLICABLE

When bringing an innovation to market, the strategist attempts to solve a problem that carries a fundamental discontinuity: To be successful, an innovation must help market players break out of the status quo's self-sealing orbit and set in motion changes that result in an endgame with its own self-sealing orbit. Each end point of the problem is internally consistent, but the path from one to the other seems to involve a logical break somewhere along the way. Up to a point, reinforcing network effects pull the player back to the initial status quo, but beyond that point, the journey becomes easier. The same network effects now attract the players to a new destination.

Clearly, beyond this transition point of critical mass, the benefits to switching outweigh the costs in the mind of each player making the switch. Part of this benefit-cost calculation is based on the belief—and, possibly, knowledge—that a critical mass has switched as well. If so, switching is indeed a best choice, and a new equilibrium is confirmed.

A strategist has four approaches for overriding the inevitable discontinuity in bringing an innovation to market and accumulating the necessary critical mass. Each approach has a measure of risk associated with it. None works in all circumstances. The innovator's strategic challenge, therefore, is to know how to choose the best approach in any given situation.

Experience suggests that, at the practical level, an innovator should think about this challenge as a problem of innovation *diffusion*, that is, the inducement of a switch in the behavior of players along the critical path to an endgame, which in turn gives way to further switching that favors the innovation's adoption. Everett Rogers introduced the classic framework for looking at diffusion.[11] He delineates five attributes that broadly determine how innovations diffuse in a market. In the following list, I have updated these criteria to reflect the additional burdens placed on innovations, since they must penetrate an interconnected market and disrupt entrenched equilibrium behavior.

- **Relative advantage:** Is the innovation better than the status quo? Is it better than competing alternatives? Is there a sufficiently compelling set of benefits to motivate players on the critical path to switch their choices in its favor, given their expectations about how other players will behave?

- **Compatibility:** How well does the innovation complement other products the consumers are using? Must they switch away from other products that they currently use? Is it interoperable? Is the cost of integrating it with other products in use relatively low?

- **Simplicity:** How simple is it to explain the benefits of the innovation? How straightforward are they? How many market connections are necessary to distribute the innovation if its benefits are to be realized?

- **"Trialability":** Are there opportunities to experience the innovation and its benefits before a party decides to adopt it?

- **Observability:** Are the innovation's benefits in the line of sight of future adopters? Can they observe the benefits enjoyed by earlier adopters? Can it be passed on to others by earlier adopters? Are the players interconnected with earlier adopters in ways that make it easier for them to learn about the innovation?

The criteria offer a guide, all else being the same, for how much resistance to a given innovation's diffusion potential we could expect. The higher an innovation scores on these criteria, the less will be the resistance. The innovation's performance on these criteria also offers a way to choose between the various multiplier mechanisms.

To begin with, an innovation will unquestionably rate low on relative advantage. In the early stages of the campaign, the network effects will almost always favor the status quo and put an innovation in a position of disadvantage. With the remaining criteria in mind, consider the following decision process:

1. First, determine if the innovation does well on the compatibility criterion. If it does, then the complementing mechanism would be applicable. Compatibility assures the potential to find a complementary relationship with the status quo.

2. Alternatively, suppose that the innovation does not meet the compatibility criterion. As long as the innovation scores well on simplicity, trialability, and observability, the infecting mechanism can be applied. Under such circumstances, the innovation already has several characteristics to do well in the market and leverage its connectedness properties to multiply by infecting the ever-increasing swathes of the market.

3. Now suppose that the innovation at the very least meets the simplicity criterion. In this case, the strategist can consider the coordinated incentives mechanism. This mechanism suggests that an innovator can approach a focused set of players to align their incentives appropriately. In the absence of simplicity,

the ability of one of these player's actions to influence the choice factor of another becomes muddled by the difficulty in communicating the benefits of adoption.

4. Finally, if the innovation does not meet any of the criteria, the hub mechanism remains the only option.

MULTIPLIER EFFECTS: MECHANISMS FOR TUNNELING TO A VISION

The campaign for getting an innovation to market begins with a decision on which endgame to pursue. With this endgame as the primary reference point, we must then create the mechanism that breaks out of the status quo and gets the market to the endgame.

Above all other considerations, this mechanism must bring about systemic change—but with focused effort that can have ripple effects into the rest of the system. The problem before the innovator is challenging both because a whole network of players has to recoordinate, and because the innovator must restrain the tendency to exert control across the whole network and risk having its resources spread too thinly.

An important point worth noting is the fundamental principle of co-evolution of the future with a wide class of players, which does not necessarily call for the presence of a physical information network. Although the examples in the book so far have involved information-intensive innovations and information networks, interconnectivity is a fact of all modern markets. The conclusions here, therefore, apply broadly to all kinds of products that attempt to penetrate such markets. Palm or Adobe Acrobat may be among the more memorable, high-profile new products, but other, less glamorous products and services must also observe the principle of co-evolution.

For example, the best-selling toothbrush in the United States in 2001 was the Crest SpinBrush. It came to market on the back of a coordinated incentives mechanism. What, you may ask, could be innovative in toothbrushes? The SpinBrush cost five dollars to the consumer, whereas most competing electric toothbrushes cost ten times as much. This difference represented an innovation not just in the production process but also in business processes. The innovators, John Osher and three other entrepreneurs, synchronized three essential interconnected players' interests. Two of these players provided access to wide networks. First there was an enabler, Procter & Gamble, with its Crest brand and powerful marketing and production capabilities, eager to win back market share lost in toothbrushes to Colgate. The second player was a major distributor, such as Wal-Mart, interested in low-priced, fast-selling items. Finally, through the wide reach of the first two players, the buyers were sufficiently intrigued by an electric toothbrush, provided it was priced close enough to ordinary toothbrushes to be worth the try.

A few key choices (keeping production and marketing costs down to retain the five-dollar price point, a "Try Me" feature in the packaging, etc.) seemed to have been enough to give rise to a business model with appropriately aligned motivations for all three players. For Procter & Gamble, the SpinBrush provided a much needed best-selling branded innovation, which proved attractive for Wal-Mart as well, given its high-volume sales and low price. The success of the SpinBrush goes a long way in proving that synchronizing the interests of the network of pivotal players makes good sense even when there is no physical network in sight.[12]

IN SUMMARY, then, to build Shimon Peres' "tunnels" to the vision of your endgame, you must bring along an entire network to the destination. You do so by putting the very linkages of networks to work as part of the campaign. In looking for the best ways to get there, resist the temptation to focus

your efforts to change on only a part of the wider interconnected system, or to attempt to transform the system in one fell
swoop. We have seen creativity and innovation in devising
mechanisms that involve selective interventions and have multiplier effects, even in supposedly lowly products, such as
toothbrushes. In other words: Avoid tunnel vision in the search
for finding ways to affect the system; make use of the system's
interconnections and leverage them.

Chapter Six

DIVIDING UP THE MIDDLEGAME

Deterrence: A process that goes beyond the rational.

—Unclassified 1995 Pentagon document

THE PATH TO ENDGAME conjures up scenes of carnage and glory, a chessboard with the remaining pieces closing in on a beleaguered monarch. The "grand masters" of earlier chapters, Adobe's Warnock and Hotmail's Bhatia, must have felt, at various points in their respective campaigns, that they were moving pieces into an elaborate configuration on an invisible game board. But their tactics were far from a black versus white face-off. As their stories made clear, they were engaging in a game with many players and not all of whom were playing for the other side. Many were enablers; many had mixed interests in the innovation's success; many were involved in a passive way. And then, of course, there were those who would have the most to lose from the innovation's success and could unambiguously claim to be the innovator's competitors.

To get a measure of how complicated the relationships on the innovation game board can be, consider the predicament of the NC's steward, Larry Ellison. As described in chapter 4,

IBM was a key member of the NC coalition. As a major PC OEM, it was also one of the biggest defenders of the status quo. And, for a while, one of IBM's projects was to build an NC rival, the NetPC, which was the Microsoft-sponsored insurance policy in case the PC status quo was disrupted.[1]

The interactions that interested the grand masters were messy in more ways than one. Given a fragmented cast of players, an innovator's campaign needs to build on a few points of intervention, which will provide leverage and multiplier effects elsewhere. If successful, this all adds up to the desired endgame.

To successfully enlist other players to create the path to a preferred endgame, an innovation must share the benefits from its adoption. Specifically, it must share them with players en route—in what can be called the *middlegame*. The most important of these middlegame decisions arise at the points of direct contact between innovator and the acting agent of influence with the rest of the system. The role of such agents is to spread the motivation to change behavior into other parts of the network. In this chapter, I focus on the tactical choices an innovator faces in deciding how future value is to be divided among these agents. The tactics range from negotiation to competition and could result in collaboration, noncooperation, or outright merger. Choosing such tactics constitutes the third critical step in the campaign.

We will first look at the various tactical options as seen from the innovator's point of view, the relationships between the options, and the order in which they ought to be considered. Then we will study some examples in an industry that, like few others, epitomizes both the tactics and the slow pace of fast change: broadband telecommunications.

Projections of the broadband experience point to an impressive array over time of new applications in the home, in the office, in automobiles, and practically everywhere else. The industry working to bring this experience to life has been busy creating the necessary infrastructure, while waiting for the industry's preferred endgame to come within sight.

The major players have followed four distinct approaches en route to this broadband endgame. Each approach has led to brilliant tactical successes along the way. Middlegame success, however, is no guarantee of the final outcome. Uncertainty can throw a wrench into the most brilliant tactics, a subject I shall reserve for chapter 7.

TACTICAL OPTIONS FOR INTERACTION

When considering the options for dealing with agents of influence, an innovator must remember that the negotiations essential to the campaign may come to involve a wide range of players. Some are likely to be competitors vying for access to the same network and for much the same reasons as the innovator's. Also, an innovator must remember that such competition may not be a bad thing. There are informational benefits to having competing bids, which provide benchmarks for assessing the value of access to the network. That said, the innovator's goal in this context is not simply to work one's way up in price until the other bidder concedes and the agent accepts. I will, instead, propose to develop a mind-set for the innovator to take an active role in influencing the moves of others so that the outcome is perceived as a win-win.

Win-win, which is used quite frequently in everyday negotiation, describes a situation in which two parties to an interaction are better off compared with the next-best option available to each of them. In the current context of interconnectedness, we can take this meaning further. An innovator should strive for an outcome in which the competing bidder wins as well. In other words, the competitor's choice to withdraw is better than a choice to compete and continue bidding. Such a win-win-win situation is, for all practical purposes, a tactical equilibrium between three parties: Each considers its choice in the negotiated outcome the best choice among the feasible alternatives, given what it expects the other parties to choose. In other words, the core principle that drives the innovator's overall campaign and acts as its strategic anchor points is also the principle that defines the desirable endgame in its focused tactical interactions with the agents of influence. A fundamental advantage of targeting such an endgame is the relative stability of the outcome, which helps reduce the risks to the innovator going forward into the rest of the network.

How do you achieve this tactical equilibrium? The key, of course, is to make the negotiated agreement with an agent more attractive to all parties than any alternative that each of them could achieve through its own actions. Several tactical options directed at both sets of players—the agents and the competitors—can steer the interaction. The following tactical options are not mutually exclusive; they should ideally be used in combination—but in a specific order.

- Discover terms of trade
- Create parallel alternatives
- Signal toughness of intent
- Commit to process boundaries

The basic principle behind this set of options is the search for different ways to limit the choices of each of the remaining parties and, simultaneously, to expand one's own choice set. Anyone who has engaged in some form of negotiation has reached into this set of tactics at one time or another. My purpose here is to provide a framework in which to establish and consider the full complement of options, particularly for the innovator attempting to make headway in a connected world. The innovator's objective is to converge on a deal that represents a viable equilibrium, a best choice for all. Since the choices of the various parties are interrelated, the innovator's actions in influencing any party's choice will affect the rest.

With such a range of tactics, where does an innovator begin? An excellent place to start is by exploring the most cooperative of solutions—discovering terms of trade—where a simple act of exchange is beneficial to all, compared with the next best alternative. This tactic is based on an expectation that, by expanding the choice set of each party, an innovator can reach an outcome that each party prefers to the alternatives. A cooperative solution has other benefits. It can help an innovator get to a desired outcome faster and with less friction among the players, which may also make the outcome more sustainable in the long term.

If cooperation is not sufficient to achieve equilibrium, you have to turn to noncooperative tactics, which are variations on the theme of expanding your own choice set while convincing the other parties that their own choice set is constrained. The four tactical options from the preceding list are progressively noncooperative. There is invariably some value lost in groping toward an agreement in a noncooperative way. That is why it makes sense to explore the options in the order given. Only if one option does not appear to be viable should you consider the next one—perhaps in combination with earlier ones.

DISCOVER TERMS OF TRADE

Negotiations have often been compared to dividing a pie, a problem that has inspired many theoretical solutions oriented toward notions of fairness, or just division. Some experts on the subject offer principles that help determine a fair division based on norms acceptable in the particular milieu in which the division is being conducted.[2] Others offer suggestions on how the parties might themselves arrive at an allocation considered acceptable and, therefore, fair by each party.[3]

Even so, pie division inherently remains a zero-sum game: One party's loss is the other's gain. Frequently, the default assumption in any negotiation is that it is a zero-sum game as well. Indeed, in interactions between innovator and agent, the parties involved usually make the assumption that they are locked into such a head-on collision. An innovator worries that it will give up too much value to the agent, which in turn feels that it must squeeze as much of its own share of the value before striking a deal.

A zero-sum framing of an interaction is usually detrimental to an innovator's objective. Even if the innovator wins the auction for access to the agent, it may end up winning at a high cost, which ultimately destroys value. Instead, the first of the four options suggests that we look for terms of trade that enable an exchange that benefits all parties. As a result, some situations could involve mutually beneficial trade in which one party's gain is not necessarily another's loss.

How do you find the terms of trade that lead to equilibrium? In most dealings with an agent, some creative exploration may lead you to discover multiple dimensions of the deal being pursued. Each of these dimensions is valued differently by the individual parties. Once the parties mutually recognize the existence of more than one dimension, you have the opportunity to discover the terms of trade that benefit both. After such a trade is done, all parties are better off. The idea is simple: One party gives up disproportionately along a dimension about which it cares less in order to gain disproportionately along another dimension about which it cares more.

To continue with the pie-division analogy, this is the equivalent of discovering that one of the two participants really likes the crust whereas the other does not care. In this case, the one that prefers crust gets a share with a disproportionate amount of crust; the other gets a larger absolute share in return. The result is that conflict is avoided and both participants are better off. An extreme version of this agreement would be if one likes only crust and the other hates it. Such a situation would make sharing even easier.

Although we can easily imagine the potential for mutually beneficial exchange between innovator and agent, the principle can go further. Such win-win opportunities for trade can also be found between an innovator and a competing bidder. The innovator can offer something that the competitor values, and in return, the competitor acquiesces in the auction.

We have to be careful, of course: The existence of such tradable dimensions is not always guaranteed. The main point is that, in practice, too many interactions tend to focus on a single measure of benefit — share of profits, control, and so forth. Such a mind-set can end up destroying value by delaying the agreement and making it potentially less stable. You have to work hard to discover additional dimensions of value and then be willing to trade them.

A Route Through Cable to the Broadband Endgame

At one time, AT&T was the one-stop shop for both innovator and agent in the U.S. telecommunications industry. Since the company's first breakup in 1984, AT&T had both acquired and divested itself of several pivotal capabilities as it searched for the right path to a favorable endgame. Near the close of 2001, it merged its cable TV and consumer service unit, AT&T Broadband, with a rival, Comcast, to create a cable powerhouse. The $72 billion deal was remarkable for its size and for the short time that had elapsed since AT&T had pursued and spectacularly won an agent in the deal that gave rise to the entity AT&T Broadband. No less remarkable, AT&T had wrested the agent from a competing suitor. And that competitor was none other than Comcast itself.[4]

To trace the story, we must go back to the mid-1990s, when many players in the telecommunications business were setting out on a journey toward a broadband endgame. In this endgame, a variety of bandwidth-hogging online applications would be transmitted to business and residential consumers over broadband (high-capacity) networks. The applications would range from communication to entertainment to security as well as educational and business exchanges. An explosion of telecommunications capacity was under way. Billions of dollars of investment were literally being buried underground in the form of fiber-optic networks. Despite the enormity of the network, every interested player had its eye on a crucial weak link in the system: the "last mile" into the consumer's home. It would be too disruptive and too expensive to complete this part of the network with newly laid optical fiber. Without the completion of this link, however, the billions of dollars of investment being made elsewhere was unlikely to pay off. Any player that was first in controlling the last mile would almost surely have the ability to charge the others an extraordinary rent.

Many last-mile solutions, such as DSL, focused on wires already going into consumers' homes. Another solution, through the coaxial cable of the cable TV companies, already reached many residential consumers and, with some basic retrofitting, could provide the bandwidth needs of most of the emerging applications. Naturally, every player with an eye on the broadband endgame was taking a deep interest in the players in the cable TV industry. It was against this backdrop that Comcast, itself a leading cable player with a $1 billion investment from Microsoft, was ready to make a play for another, more pivotal, player in the cable industry. Microsoft, for its part, was eager to find avenues to have its Windows CE software run the cable set-top boxes that might become the controllers of broadband content. Comcast was interested in becoming a leader in the delivery of broadband applications to the home. The agent in question was MediaOne, a high-speed Internet access provider.

With Microsoft's backing, Comcast made a $54 billion offer to acquire MediaOne. Comcast's announcement became a public declaration of the opening of a de facto auction. Its interest conveyed an instant signal to other interested parties that MediaOne was a valuable asset — and that the asset was "in play." The exact value of MediaOne's pivotal position had been signaled by the opening bid. This would make it a tad easier for the next mover to set a counterbid.

The next mover was AT&T. It had its eye on the broadband prize because it too was seeking a direct, high-speed way into the home. A cable company's wires, high speed or not, were a way for AT&T to offer local service bundled with its core long-distance service and lower its costs by reducing the access fees it was charged by the regional local phone companies. With these benefits in mind, AT&T was a highly motivated second bidder. Its counteroffer of $62.5 billion for MediaOne represented a hefty premium over Comcast's opening bid.

Comcast had started with a high bid itself, apparently without fully anticipating the auction that might ensue. It now needed a few well-heeled friends, or it had to prepare to withdraw. The company went back to its old ally and part owner, Microsoft, and to others that might want to pip AT&T at the post. Comcast picked AOL, the Internet service provider, as a potential backer in its counterchallenge to AT&T.

Meanwhile, MediaOne was more than flattered by the attention. It announced its readiness to entertain the competing bids. With a formal auction started, the risks for AT&T were high. With bids followed by counterbids, the price of access could rise dramatically. The chances of such an eventuality had become higher with the ongoing speculation about AOL's interest in helping Comcast. No matter which side won, the deal with MediaOne now promised to be a costly one.

AT&T faced the two classic choices confronting any participant in an auction: Prepare to work up the path of escalation after Comcast returns with another bid, or withdraw for fear of overpaying for MediaOne's assets. Instead, AT&T took a creative third path: The company began exploring terms of trade with the competing side. Specifically, it started by constraining Comcast's set of choices by approaching its chief ally, Microsoft.

Approaching Microsoft was a calculated tactic on the part of AT&T. Despite its heft in the computer industry, Microsoft would be somewhat reluctant to get involved in a full-scale bidding war against a customer as important as AT&T.

Moreover, AT&T was clearly determined to move into the cable TV arena, which would open up additional sales opportunities for Microsoft, particularly for its struggling CE product. AT&T's overture to restrict Comcast's choice set paid off. Microsoft agreed not to join Comcast's bid and was ready to switch camps. It took a 3 percent stake in AT&T and, in exchange, obtained a guarantee that its operating system and applications software would be used in AT&T's cable and Internet offerings in the cable set-top box. AT&T offered Microsoft a guaranteed sales opportunity and earned Microsoft's investment and a weakening of the threat of Comcast's competitive bid in return.

Comcast's hopes of obtaining a clear commitment of support from AOL had dimmed, as AOL considered whether to go up against AT&T and Microsoft without a clear payoff. Given the might of the opposite side, few other candidate investors were willing to join Comcast in a counterbid. With its options dramatically reduced, Comcast became open to trade with AT&T and to finding a situation preferable to continuing its bid for MediaOne.

The strategy worked. A tactical equilibrium had been reached. Comcast declared that it would drop out of the bidding for MediaOne. In exchange, it received 750,000 cable subscribers from AT&T, an option to gain an additional 1.25 million in the future, and guaranteed preferential terms when it negotiated to resell AT&T-branded telephone service. For AT&T, the winning of a major agent of influence such as MediaOne was a key step in establishing its ability to propagate broadband services to a wide base of customers. Comcast's chairman declared the outcome a win-win. Because MediaOne was acquired by the highest bidder at a price that exceeded Comcast's original bid, MediaOne benefited as well.

By expanding the dimensions along which value is created, a strategist discovers ways to trade and create value for all parties to an interaction. For example, AT&T found the terms of trade in a three-way deal: with Microsoft and with Comcast. It won MediaOne at a lower price than it would have had to pay had the auction continued.

CREATE PARALLEL ALTERNATIVES

Two crucial issues to be resolved — even if you can find the dimensions to trade on — are how much you ought to give up and what is an acceptable demand from the opposite side. After all, the decision to trade must be negotiated, which means that both parties must feel convinced that there is no better option available to them. If one of the parties is to reject an offer on the table, it must have an alternative set of options that is better able to convince the others that such a choice is feasible. This has several implications.

The first implication is that the innovator — and its counterparty on the opposite side of the interaction — must learn about the alternatives to reaching an agreement with each other. In other words, you must pursue other interactions and opportunities in parallel or be prepared to do so. This is important even if you know that it is not in your best interest to choose one of the other alternatives.

The second implication is that whatever the alternatives turn out to be, they have to be credibly communicated to the counterparties. There has to be some observable, public element in the alternatives that you pursue or other ways of verifying the existence of the parallel interactions. The goal, of course, is to create a sufficiently high likelihood in the counterparty's mind that you can indeed pursue such alternatives.

As we have seen, the value of a deal with an agent is hard to measure. This value affects the terms of trade that would, conceivably, be agreed upon either by the innovator and the agent or by the competing bidders. This also means that the value created by a trade is hard to measure. There is a need for appropriate external benchmarks. The pursuit of alternatives helps bring such benchmarks to the table and set bounds on the demands made by either side. These bounds help the parties understand the terms beyond which it makes sense for at least one of the parties to walk away.

Those who study the principles of bargaining have emphasized the importance of such alternatives, calling them, variously, a disagreement point, a threat point, or a BATNA (best alternative to negotiated agreement).[5] A distinction that I would make between the present suggestion and these other approaches is that the alternative options are treated very much as a part of the strategic variables, as opposed to being considered a fixed alternative to negotiating an agreement. This suggests that the dynamics of the primary interaction between innovator and agent are linked to the dynamics of what is going on in any parallel path the innovator is following.

The Undersea Route to the Broadband Endgame

If one significant bottleneck to a global broadband infrastructure is the last mile into the consumer's home, then the other has to be the longest of long-haul links that connect continents. The first modern transcontinental fiber-optic cables laid across the Atlantic Ocean were filled up long before they were expected to do so. Since then many new undersea networks have been developed.

While the transatlantic route was the central focus of activity in creating new undersea network capacity, it was becoming clear to certain forward-looking players that much underserved demand would reside on the other side of the globe. Across the trans-Pacific route, particularly for traffic to and from the rapidly growing Chinese economy, a new undersea system could help unlock a potentially explosive volume of traffic—both plain old telephony and broadband. This was an endgame visualized by the Chinese telecommunications authorities, who went about searching for the agent that would help them get there.[6]

A cable system was ultimately built between China and the United States at a cost of $950 million, and it stretches for sixteen thousand miles. This system initially went into service in January 2000 and is co-owned by a consortium that includes China Telecom, AT&T, and a dozen other telecommunications players, including Kokusai Denshi Denwa (KDD) of Japan, SBC Communications, and Telstra of Australia. Each has an equal stake in the entity. This arrangement was, however, not meant to be this way when the negotiations—typical for complex projects such as these—started back in 1994. The somewhat crowded consortium grew out of an aggressive application of the create-parallel-alternatives tactic by the Chinese negotiators.

In the early 1990s, China was emerging as a global superpower. Yet most of its telecommunications traffic went through the territory of its erstwhile political—and present economic—rival, Japan. The Chinese were keen to have their own system with direct fiber-optic connectivity to the biggest source and destination of its future traffic, the United States. With the forthcoming boom in broadband applications, there was also a concern about creating enough capacity and direct connectivity to ensure that China could participate as a major player in that outcome.

There was a problem, though, in putting the system in place. The Chinese had very little leverage with the relevant network of players on the critical path. The undersea cable-laying industry was—and still is—the domain of an elite few. Two out of the three major players were AT&T and Japan's KDD. As the major owners and operators of cable systems worldwide, they shared 40 percent of Asia's cable capacity between them.

AT&T would be a natural agent of influence for China. It also had the potential to be truly pivotal. AT&T, with its multiple roles—as a cable-laying and network-planning company, a service provider, a technology and product provider, and a potential source of capital—might have so much leverage in the interactions that any final agreement might give it a disproportionate share of the value. At least that was what it looked like from the Chinese point of view. There was early evidence to suggest the likelihood of such an asymmetric relationship. The Chinese were chafing at AT&T's proposed project plan, which included a routing through Japan, and at AT&T's promotion of its own cable-laying subsidiary as a prime contractor. The only player at the table other than AT&T was KDD, a Japanese company, which did not add to the comfort of the Chinese, given their political concerns.

With this as backdrop, the Chinese decided to find ways to expand their own choice set by seeking alternatives. They also wanted to demonstrate to AT&T that they were doing so. The idea was to encourage a broad set of participants to come to the negotiation table to discuss options for how the cable system would be built. Public statements in the early rounds of negotiations said it all: "We want to engage as many companies as possible on an equal basis." The declarations were intended to send a message both to the incumbent pivotal players and to others that would see this as an invitation to qualify as an alternative.

The plan paid off, particularly since it was well timed with transformations taking place in the U.S. telecommunications industry structure. The Telecommunications Act of 1996 was about to free up the local phone companies, the Baby Bells, and allow them to compete in new markets including international telecommunications. One such player, SBC Communications, was in the process of simultaneously eyeing the international opportunity and an acquisition of Pacific Telesis, another Baby Bell company. The two opportunities also came together nicely in the China situation, since the primary destination of communications from China would be into Pacific Telesis territory.

With China's encouragement, despite little experience in the undersea cable business, SBC entered the fray with its own competing vision of the U.S.–China project plan. The Chinese negotiators talked to both parties simultaneously, using offers from one set of discussions in the other set of talks and allowing "controlled leaks" of information. This was a perfect illustration of the concept of parallel interactions discussed earlier, with each interaction defining the bounds of the other.

The alternatives did not stop with SBC, however. A raft of new players was brought to the table, each interaction acting as a disciplining device for the remaining ones—especially the one with AT&T. Among the other players were MCI, Sprint, and Nippon Telegraph and Telephone. Despite its original dominance in the undersea cable industry, the AT&T/KDD coalition was no longer in a position of setting the rules of play and demanding a disproportionate share of the value.

The result was that, as more parties were invited to join the dialogue, the center of gravity in the negotiations was always with the Chinese negotiators. For any proposal from the agents, there was a credible counterproposal because of the expanded choice set. This also served to restrict the choice set of the agents. Ultimately, the parties reached a tactical equilibrium: The number of players that could participate in the system with equal shares and rights would stand at fourteen— a far cry from the original, two-party discussions between the AT&T/KDD coalition and the Chinese officials.

As observed earlier, the tactical options can—and, whenever possible, should—be combined. Even though their original position had been significantly diminished by the invitations extended to the additional parties, AT&T and KDD did celebrate some victories. In exchange for their diminished status, they uncovered new dimensions for terms of trade with the Chinese. Although the initiative was motivated, for example, at the start by a desire to bypass Japan, KDD had remained keen on a landing point on its home country. The final plans for the cable system included a drop in Okinawa, Japan.

SIGNAL TOUGHNESS OF INTENT

An innovator must bid against competitors as if it were engaging in a virtual auction to win a deal with the agent of influence. Now, the whole point of an auction is that even though, in principle, you may be prepared to bid as high as the value the prize holds for you, the price you actually pay just has to beat the highest bid beyond which all competing bidders have bowed out. Thus, a key to retaining a higher share of the value is to convince the competitors to bow out earlier. If some competitors' bids exceed the maximum you are willing to pay, then, of course, you have lost the agent because of market forces. On the other hand, if you believe that you value the prize potentially more highly than the competition does, then it pays to make investments in communicating this information earlier so that the other bidders drop out before the costs of your victory escalate further.

Communication with another bidder is hard enough because of the natural barriers associated with competitive rivalry. The agent will also be inclined to reinforce these barriers by keeping the competing bidders separated and preventing them from communicating and discovering terms of trade with each other. After all, communication among competing bidders would only result in a lower-winning bid if they agree to "tone it down" or if bidders drop out early. There is, however, a more subtle challenge in communicating with other bidders. You need to communicate the message "I am tougher than you are." The desired outcome is to cause a competitor to back off since it feels it has no chance of winning. To be effective, this message must be communicated in a credible way. Otherwise, it would be easy for the competitor to dismiss it.

One way to distinguish a credible message from cheap talk and empty bluster is to invest in a signal. To be effective, the signal must cost you money and must communicate your intent and commitment. The objective of making the signal expensive is to send a message: "I am tough and willing to spend money to convince others of that truth." There is another side to the signal. It must also be easily "read" or understood by the party on the receiving end. Otherwise, you may make an investment without getting any value out of it. Indeed, many signals have little intrinsic benefit other than that of sending a message to others.

Although the notion of a signal may seem a little abstract, we invest in them and utilize them constantly to relay information in our day-to-day lives. Common examples of signals include the offer of product warranties or money-back guarantees, obtaining degrees from reputable educational institutions (even if similar education can be obtained at lower cost from elsewhere), overpreparing on seemingly trivial details to make a good first impression in interviews and sales meetings—the list goes on.[7] Each of these involves a cost, which the recipient of the signal understands. Although the cost should not wipe out the gains that you would enjoy from a competitor's dropping out early, your willingness to commit resources is an important message to the other party about your true intent. In the process, you are affecting a competing bidder's perception of its own choice set, and its perception of how it compares with your choice set. A signal of toughness is intended to give competing parties the sense that their choices are more limited than yours and steers them toward a best choice where they consider dropping out.

Although signals involve investment, the investments have to be bounded. Take, for example, the notion of signaling through product warranties. For the signal to be a viable proposition, only a small fraction of buyers of the product should make use of the warranty. The investment required by the signal must be relatively small compared to the increase in sales of the product due to the message conveyed by the warranty.

Also, signals come in many forms. In a warranty, the signal is in the form of a contractual promise to take certain actions in case of some contingency. An alternative form of signaling common in competitive bidding situations is the practice of *jump bidding*: signals of toughness sent through big jumps in the counterbid to an opponent's bid or through the offer of abnormally large premiums to a bid on a targeted acquisition. If successful, such expensive signals pay off because the winner deters the competition. In a competitive bidding situation, it could limit the escalation of bids and prevent the signaling party from having to pay an even higher price. Still another form of signaling may involve *cheap talk*: preannouncements to the media about forthcoming moves or products, or the practice used by some in the technology industry and known as vaporware (see chapter 2). In sum, it requires substantial creativity to create effective signals.

The Local Loop Route to the Broadband Endgame

The best of all possible outcomes to an attempt to send a costly signal is, of course, to have the tactic succeed without the signal actually costing you anything when the dust settles. This lucky result could happen even if you were prepared to invest in the signal at the outset. If this seems improbable, consider the case of the quest for US West.[8] Two suitors went after the regional Bell holding company that operated local phone services in the mountain states. Although both suitors had started out with a focus on the long-haul piece of the broadband infrastructure, US West was viewed as a pivotal agent in getting broadband connectivity to the homes and businesses of the customers. One suitor sent a powerful, costly signal of toughness. It ended up with the prize and did not have to make added investments in the signal after all, despite its commitment to paying an extraordinarily high premium for the signal.

The competing suitors in this case were Global Crossing and Qwest. Both were new players in the industry, at the forefront of building out fiber-optic networks to transport broadband traffic over long distances. One came by land and the other by sea. Qwest had utilized its ownership of railroad rights-of-way to build fiber rings within the continental United States; Global Crossing was developing undersea cable systems connecting continents. Both had facilities optimized for high-speed data and future broadband applications. And both had a common deficiency: They lacked a presence in the last mile to the customer, the so-called local loop.

Although building their local loops would have been expensive, it would also have been equally disadvantageous to strike deals with multiple regional companies. Both were in search of an agent that would give them access to a wide swath of customers. In March 1999, Global Crossing took its first steps toward extending into the local loop: It made an $11.2 billion bid for Frontier, an independent local telephone company based in Rochester, NY. Two months later, it followed up with a $35 billion bid for US West and raised its bid for Frontier to $12.9 billion.

June 1999, enter Qwest and its CEO, Joseph Nacchio, who already had a bit of a reputation for toughness. Like the Comcast and AT&T situation, the Global Crossing proposal simply acted as an opening bid and a benchmark for the next mover. Qwest's entry was marked by a sweeping move: It declared that it would top both of Global Crossing's bids. On the face of it, this seemed like an ordinary auction, in which the second bidder counterbids on the opening price by offering an added premium. It was, however, a little odd for Qwest to target both the prizes. With its headquarters in Colorado, there would be a natural logic to its bid for US West. The question that came up in many analysts' minds was, Why go after Frontier as well and complicate the acquisition?

An explanation for this peculiar double bid was that Frontier was not a serious target for Qwest. The move was a potentially expensive signal to Global Crossing's management of the seriousness of its pursuit of US West. Global Crossing tried several avenues to bypass a head-to-head auction. For example, it appealed to Governor Bill Owens of Colorado to endorse its bid for US West and filed with the Securities and Exchange Commission (SEC) to win shareholder approval of its bid for Frontier.

Despite all these efforts, Qwest's seriousness in pursuing the prize to the bitter end seemed to become clearer as time wore on. Despite negotiations between the bidders, Qwest showed no intention of stepping aside. In fact, it showed every intention of escalating its campaign. Finally, convinced that Qwest was truly going to fight on, Global Crossing ended the contest in July. US West was merged with Qwest for $35 billion. With its signal value now used up, Qwest relinquished its bid for Frontier. Global Crossing acquired Frontier for its original $11.2 billion without further bid escalation by Qwest. In return, Global Crossing reduced the deal-breaking penalty on US West, further easing its acquisition by Qwest.

The game was won at the opening bid with little penalty. The key to this freezing of the auction was the cleverly signaled intent conveyed in Qwest's surprise and counterintuitive double bid. It was clear that the message had been read clearly by the receiving party. "The word I got was that they [Qwest] were going to keep this up at any price. We were not willing to be the any-price company," acknowledged Robert Annunziata, CEO of Global Crossing, on the day each company walked away with its prize. Both parties made a best choice from their available set of choices, given the information they had at the time. An equilibrium had been achieved.

COMMIT TO PROCESS BOUNDARIES

If successful, signaling can bring an innovator closer to an early agreement with the agent of influence. It is, nonetheless, a somewhat risky move; you may make the investment and the message may not get across as intended or may not result in the desired action. In the previous example, Qwest could have been put in the position of having to absorb both US West at a much higher price and Frontier as well, without really intending to win both.[9]

An alternative to bearing this risk is to set the rules of the game by which the various parties have to play by setting boundaries on how the process of interaction unfolds. There are many ways in which this can be done. You could set a time deadline for resolution and commit to walking away if the deal is still in negotiation. Alternatively, you could make a take-it-or-leave-it offer — a firm bid beyond which you are not prepared to negotiate. Like signaling, boundary setting is intended to affect the perceptions of the other parties about their choice set. If they feel that their choice set is constrained by the boundaries you have placed on them, the interaction will move to equilibrium faster.

In general, in any dynamic setting, a good strategist will set bounds beyond which it simply does not make good business sense to play. These limits can be based on analysis done beforehand to define an outer bound, say, on the budget that an innovator can expend to win over an agent. The boundary I refer to here, though, is of a different kind: It is a tactical bound. The purpose is to force a resolution by betting that, as a matter of natural risk aversion, players are not inclined to losing an attractive offer "in the hand" for a better offer still "in the bush." This tactic is ideal when you are fairly sure that the others have exhausted their ability to get to the desired outcome, and some form of a deadline or final offer will produce a favorable result.

This approach does carry some risks. The other party may not believe that you will actually enforce the boundary conditions. You have to demonstrate a credible commitment to doing so — which is quite hard to do. An example of such commitment is a contract with another agent that is activated in the event that your deadline has passed with no resolution.

But although establishing credibility is important, you may pursue this tactic even if you cannot demonstrate proof of your commitment. As long as the other players have a preference for the offer in the hand, they may be sufficiently fearful of losing an attractive deal and may be sufficiently averse to taking on that risk. The trick is to make the deal in the hand seem even more attractive to the other party.

The Long-Distance Route to the Broadband Endgame

In the summer of 1996, the U.S. long-distance telecommunications industry was in the middle of a major transformation, with forces of change coming from many directions. With deregulation in the air, the established long-distance players were preparing for an onslaught from the regional Bell companies. Global alliances were beginning to form. Unknown companies, some with plans hatched on napkins, were on the verge of making their presence felt. Competitors were converging on an endgame whose details had not become clear. What was clear, however, was that the status quo was about to change—and change dramatically.

With the air thick with anticipation, the first significant event arrived when the United Kingdom's British Telecom, BT, made a move to dislodge the equilibrium. It made an offer to buy MCI, the second-largest U.S. long-distance player, for $24 billion. This was only the beginning of more moves to come. BT's offer for MCI triggered a chain of events that led to the emergence of a significant new player on the U.S. and the global stage: WorldCom, the company with the plan that began on a napkin.[10]

Shortly after the bid for MCI, BT's shareholders had second thoughts. MCI's core business of long-distance telephony in the United States was already being threatened by the potential of new entrants. New services over the Internet and data communications were right around the corner, making the bread-and-butter long-distance service even less attractive. By August 1997, BT had reconsidered the earlier bid, which the company reduced to $19 billion. This gave World-Com a reason to inject itself into the game. MCI would clearly be a pivotal player in WorldCom's campaign to become a national, if not a global, player. Its surprise $30 billion counterbid for MCI was announced on 1 October 1997.

WorldCom's huge premium over the standing bid was a jump bid—a strong signal of its intent and of keen interest in winning. If all had gone well, the process would have ended right there. The others, particularly BT and other prospective bidders, would have read the signal and would have let WorldCom walk away with MCI for the $30 billion price tag in the expectation that an auction was not winnable. In fact, BT's shareholders had already started making noises about their lack of enthusiasm for the pursuit of MCI.

Just when it seemed that the signaling tactic would be sufficient to seal WorldCom's victory, the auction expanded. WorldCom's move inspired a third bidder, GTE, to throw its hat into the ring. GTE needed a national provider to close the many gaps in its long-distance coverage, and MCI was as good a candidate for this pivotal role as any. From GTE's perspective, WorldCom's bid, far from being read as a signal of toughness, was an external validation of MCI's value. GTE's counter-counterbid was for $28 billion, all in cash.

By now, with more determined bidders in the fray, BT was increasingly interested in finding a way out. It was also in a position that could allow it to shift from being a competitor to WorldCom to the role of de facto decision maker for the agent: With a 20 percent ownership stake in the company, it was already a major shareholder in MCI.

With this new dynamic in place, it initially seemed that GTE was gaining the upper hand. BT appeared more inclined toward a merger between MCI and GTE. "There is less overlap between GTE and BT, than there is between WorldCom and BT," Sir Peter Bonfield, BT's CEO, was quoted as saying, suggesting that a partnership with GTE would in fact extend BT's reach into local telephony in the United States.[11] MCI's chairman, Bert Roberts Jr., also met with GTE's Charles Lee and urged him to raise his bid.

WorldCom clearly had to explore creative solutions—particularly in terms of winning over BT's crucial vote. It had tried the signaling approach—and that had backfired with GTE's entry at a high bid. WorldCom was not in a position to create alternatives for itself, since it was pursuing MCI and not the other way around, and MCI itself already had an alternative in GTE. WorldCom needed to find terms of trade to make its proposition significantly more attractive. For this, it focused on the original issue that had stalled BT's own pursuit of MCI—the shareholder concerns.

Given BT's business circumstances, its shareholders would have a high preference for cash. A higher cash offer in exchange for its stake in MCI had the potential of making any offer far more attractive. GTE was already willing to close an all-cash deal. In November 1997, WorldCom agreed to up the ante: It sweetened its offer to $35.6 billion in cash and stock, and around $7 billion in cash for BT's 20 percent stake, plus a $1.6 billion breakup fee. Moreover, it made certain organizational concessions. MCI's chairman, Roberts, would be chairman of the new company, and senior management positions would be secured for his team. WorldCom had demonstrated that it would be willing to work with the key decision makers. It offered to find terms to trade that would matter most to the decision makers: To MCI management it offered the chance to lead the new company, and to BT's shareholders it could offered much-needed cash. This was significantly more than what GTE had to offer—even though in dollar terms, World-Com had not raised the premium by the same order of magnitude as it had the first time it had placed its bid.

GTE, surprised by the latest bid, indicated that it would be willing to raise its offer, but would need time to do additional due diligence. And time was the one thing that WorldCom was not willing to concede on. Its generous proposal was a take-it-or-leave-it offer with an expiry date. It would be null and void if it were not accepted by a deadline of 10 November.

BT's shareholders realized that the attractive cash offer could be withdrawn after the deadline. Given the uncertainty associated with GTE's due diligence process, there was no guarantee that it would be able to match WorldCom's offer either before or after the deadline. Finally, the degree of impatience, already stretched thin, exceeded the possibility of an even better offer, or the chances that WorldCom would actually renegotiate after the deadline.

The boundary tactic worked as intended. On 9 November 1997, MCI, with BT's consent, agreed to be purchased by WorldCom.

A key element in the increasing tension that led to equilibrium was the exhaustion of BT's patience and bank of resources. BT needed to settle fast, and WorldCom found a way to force a decision. By honing in on the aspects of the deal that would help it close, WorldCom ended the destructive path of a continuing war of attrition against GTE and potentially against BT as well.

Also, as the last of the tactical options, the application in this case study illustrates how it can be used most effectively when combined with several of the earlier ones to yield the desired tactical equilibrium.

WHAT LIES BEYOND A SUCCESSFUL MIDDLEGAME

Innovation-to-market campaigns in fragmented, networked markets lean heavily on the ability to influence a few critical players. It is these players that help propagate the innovation's influence through a middlegame and bring about the wider set of changes in behaviors necessary for a successful endgame. This makes it supremely important to win the support of these agents of influence — and to do so on favorable terms. The very access that these agents provide also invites competition for the innovator. As you consider the path to an endgame, you must acknowledge that others will be attempting to create their own paths. This chapter has highlighted various approaches to managing the collaborative and competitive interactions with such players in interconnected market environments.

The tactics discussed in this chapter apply to a broad spectrum of agreements between innovator and agent, not just mergers and acquisitions (M&A), which have dominated the illustrations. Joint ventures, licensing agreements, and even implicit contracts can also provide the ideal way to lock in a deal pivotal to an innovation's success. M&A transactions are a major step whose trade-offs should be considered along with other, less risky alternatives. One study has shown that 61 percent of buyers in M&A transactions above $500 million (where buyers offered at least 15 percent of their market capitalization) destroyed shareholder value when it was measured a year after the deal closing. The average return for all buyers was 4.3 percent below that of their peers and 9.2 percent below the Standard & Poor's 500.[12] The study also found that the biggest reason that mergers do not pay off on average is because the buyers overpay. All in all, the tactics discussed in this chapter are geared toward preventing a fall into the inevitable trap of winning by overpayment.

Remarkably, every protagonist in this chapter had engineered brilliant middlegames, only to find the endgame ultimately much more elusive. Broadband adoption as a whole fell far below expectations, wiping out $2 trillion of value in the telecommunications industry in the period after these deals concluded. AT&T, as we know, eventually offered up its hard-won prize to Comcast; undersea fiber-optic networks went on to experience excess capacity and rapidly falling prices. The post-merger environment of Qwest and US West proved to be full of regret and recrimination, resulting ultimately in the departure of the deal maker Nacchio, and Bernard Ebbers, chief architect of the takeover of MCI, eventually resigned as the value of WorldCom collapsed.

Accusations and evidence of financial wrongdoing abound in the industry. This situation can partly be traced to the success of the middlegame, which had created such overblown expectations for the endgame to follow.

My purpose in this chapter was to highlight successful middlegame tactics, not successful foresight. In fact, these illustrations have served to draw our attention to the importance of uncertainty—the other side of the coin of choices made in favor of any particular endgame. This is the subject of chapter 7.

Chapter Seven

DEALING WITH UNCERTAINTY

Whatif nobody likes me?

—Shel Silverstein, *A Light in the Attic*

IBM WAS APPROACHED in 1959 by the little-known Haloid Company with a proposal to invest in a new technology for "dry copying." Upon the advice of its technology consultants, IBM took a pass. Despite the vote of no confidence from the preeminent high-technology company of the time, Haloid raised capital with support from other, less skeptical sources. It took its first product, the 914 copier, to market in 1960. Within a decade, the bet had made its way to the desired endgame. The company had revolutionized the way the printed or written page was reproduced all over the industrialized world—with the possible exception of the Soviet Union, where it was deemed illegal. Haloid had won the ultimate honor in innovation; its new name had become both noun and de facto verb: Xerox.[1]

The history of bringing innovations to market would be half as long without such bets. But there is much more to the history than bets. The market's response to innovation will inevitably be uncertain. There is good reason to find alternatives to a bold, irreversible choice until you know more.

149

Consider Xerox again. Its management was sufficiently farsighted to know that the endgame it had brought together was only a new status quo, which would invite the next generation of innovations aiming to dismantle it. Breakthroughs in the ways in which documents are reproduced and distributed would not stop with the photocopier. Xerox's follow-up strategy was to reserve options to participate in the next generation. It established the Palo Alto Research Center (PARC), a separate facility for research on information technologies and computer science. The discoveries at PARC were by no means a corporate commitment to commercializing them; they were relatively small, focused investments in R&D, which would provide managers with visibility over the horizon and an option to play in the next round.

The options that Xerox had invested in did pay off: From PARC came some of the fundamental building blocks of the modern information infrastructure. The options were, however, (famously) cashed in not by Xerox but by others. "We have always been shameless about stealing great ideas," Steve Jobs, who visited Xerox PARC in 1979, once admitted. Jobs then proceeded to reincarnate the Alto from Xerox PARC into the Apple Macintosh.[2] Apple went on to lead the reshaping of computers into the personal appliances we know today. Other Xerox options, such as the Ethernet protocol, had a profound influence on how information itself is distributed and reproduced over networks. Before long, thanks in part to changes that Xerox PARC itself had helped set in motion, the once-mighty photocopier was giving "page share" away to the laser printer. A new endgame was in sight.

As the tide was turning more quickly than most would have imagined, Xerox could not defer decisions any longer. It had already missed out on cashing in on its options in PARC; it had to find ways to participate in the next emerging endgame. The catch was that the product anchoring the previous status quo, the photocopier, was still its core. A shift of emphasis to laser printers by the company whose name was synonymous with the photocopier could send its flagship product even more quickly toward oblivion. In sum, the company had to make a bet, but Xerox also needed a way to place a lower bound on its market position in any scenario: whether the copier held its ground or if the laser printer were to rapidly displace it. The solution to which Xerox turned was to buy "insurance": an up-front investment that evened out the impact in either scenario. Xerox launched a new product line of multifunction devices, which perform *both* printing and copying functions. The devices were like an insurance policy: Join the trend toward printers without killing the copier, by binding one to the other.

In its remarkable history, Xerox has had several confrontations with innovation's perennial companion: uncertainty. The fledgling company had taken its nascent, unproven proposition to a disbelieving incumbent owner of a status quo. Having survived the rebuff and flourished, it then assumed the role of disbelieving incumbent itself. As it saw a new Xerox-less equilibrium settling in, it was placed in the difficult position of making yet another bet while preparing for protection against a worst-case scenario. Xerox had over this period invested in several innovations: the copier, the computing and networking inventions from PARC, and the multifunction device. In terms of its commitment to an endgame, Xerox had run the gamut of choices at uncertainty's table: the preemptive bet, reserving options to decide later, and buying insurance.

In this chapter, I discuss different forms of commitment to an endgame in the presence of the uncertainty about its realization. We reflect on the nature of uncertainty itself and whether it is best to prepare to react to it or to preemptively get ahead of it. Creating, thus, a commitment policy is the fourth aspect of our campaign to bring innovation to market.

During the course of an innovation campaign, uncertainty could enter at many points: when you are qualifying endgames, deciding on the right multiplier mechanism, or choosing a tactical play. At the outset of the campaign, when the endgame is being qualified and targeted, the tone for the overall commitment gets set. It is also at the outset when the uncertainty is the greatest, and so is the potential impact of making a commitment. As described earlier, an endgame would be judged on the basis of whether it satisfies the conditions of an equilibrium. Many of these conditions are predicated on *expectations* about future events or behaviors of other market players. This is what makes uncertainty so central to our discussion. Although this chapter focuses on uncertainty at the important initial point in the campaign, the framework can also be applied at subsequent stages.

Of course, the process of qualifying endgames is a key step in reducing the negative impact of uncertainty. We must nevertheless recall that the endgame being targeted is the most preferred of several plausible alternatives. One of these plausible alternatives could still be realized, despite the innovator's efforts. It is unwise not to have a plan for dealing with such possibilities. In fact, despite the best forward-looking strategy, perhaps the only thing certain about innovation's journey to market is the uncertainty that will travel with it. Our objective is to prepare for this certainty.

THE COMMITMENT DILEMMA

In our day-to-day experience, uncertainty evokes responses that may as well be polar opposites of each other. On the one hand, when pressed to make a choice in uncertain environments, our natural reaction is to want to defer making an irreversible decision until more information is available. On the other, because the choice is being made in a networked market, we might place a high premium on actively shaping the choices of others. We may need to act preemptively to establish competitive advantage or to limit the choice sets of other players and make their reactions more predictable. This calls for moving first—often with an irreversible bet.

In other words, both deferring a choice and making one preemptively are rational ways of dealing with uncertainty. The preemptive method does so by closing options; the deferral method keeps them open. Which path should be pursued at any given juncture involving uncertainty in your campaign? This is the commitment dilemma.

It may seem that buying insurance provides a bridge between the two stark choices. After all, it combines an early move with the assumption that you also make investments that offer a minimum level of "protection," regardless of the final outcome. Would it be natural to automatically seek insurance to avoid the dilemma? Not quite, since buying insurance is not always desirable; it is an expensive, up-front investment, against which the benefits have to be weighed.

How, then, can you choose between the different forms of commitment? The answer lies in developing a more robust understanding of the *strategic situation* before you—that is, the point in a campaign when the choice of a target endgame hangs in the balance. It is the difficulty in making a precise forecast of the endgame that creates uncertainty. The relation of a given situation to the endgame being targeted points to one of the three forms of commitment. In the same way that Xerox used different forms of commitment, over the course of many years, a single player can have the opportunity to try all three. This chapter offers a diagnostic framework for recognizing distinct strategic situations and the form of commitment that would be suitable to each.

Developing some such commitment policy is preferable to using the rules of thumb frequently—and indiscriminately—applied. These rules of thumb are familiar: the first-mover advantage, the importance of maintaining a high degree of flexibility, the importance of modularity. The first may underestimate the downside risk of moving early and the value of learning from others. The second and third often lead to commitments that lack needed scale, or run the risk of being preempted by a competitor. They can also restrict an innovator from taking leadership in orchestrating a visionary endgame.[3] As the following section will show, the right approach to commitment depends on a diagnosis of the strategic situation at hand.

FRAMEWORK FOR A DIAGNOSIS
OF STRATEGIC SITUATIONS

Strategic situations can be messy and complex, but they can be characterized by several intuitive criteria. These criteria bear directly on how much and how soon to commit. They give rise to a framework summarized in table 7-1.

The assessment of the strategic situation must then be mapped to the alternative forms of commitment. Let us now consider each in turn—and how performance on the various criteria would lead us to it.

MAKING THE BIG BET

A big bet is a choice that is decisive and that generally involves a high up-front investment and an irreversible commitment. After such a bet, there is little room for making adjustments for different contingencies. This means that you have to be quite sure of the benefits of making a preemptive choice and must have strong expectations about being able to steer the choices of others to follow in the desired direction.

When is such a high degree of commitment appropriate? The conditions for making such commitments are more favorable when the strategic situation rates "high" across most, if not all, of the criteria in the framework just introduced. The following section describes the logic of such commitment through a bet that stood out even in an environment abundant in big bets.

TABLE 7-1

Diagnostic Framework for a Strategic Situation

Criterion	Guiding Questions/Details
Motivation to disrupt status quo	How much added value accrues to the innovator from replacing a status quo with an alternative equilibrium, the desired endgame? In addition to the inherent benefits of the innovation's adoption, this added value draws on the inefficiencies that impose costs on the innovator in the status quo, the relative low risk of cannibalization of existing profitable businesses by the innovation, or other conflicts.
Potential for proprietary pioneering benefits	Does the innovation offer exclusive technological, economic, or knowledge advantages to the pioneer, with few spillover benefits that can be appropriated by other players that follow? Is there valuable learning by doing, whose benefits can be enjoyed and preserved for the pioneer?
Need for creation of a new network versus using a preexisting network	Does the innovator need to build a new network to implement the campaign to an endgame, or can it piggyback on an accessible, preexisting network that can provide an infrastructure of necessary relationships, complementary products, and technologies?
Signaling value	Do the innovator's actions have high potential to convey information to other players on the critical path? Can this information motivate the others to switch to behaviors consistent with getting to the endgame?
Barriers to creating limited tests	Is it possible to gauge the reaction of the market to the innovator's actions through a test or pilot that simulates a full-blown launch of the innovation without actually doing so? Are there minimum scale requirements of the innovation that prevent such tests from being truly representative or even feasible?
Leverage across the adopter network	Is the networked market such that the innovator has significant influence over a sufficiently wide segment of adopters on the critical path to the endgame? The innovator could exert such influence through agents of influence, or through a particularly effective multiplier mechanism.

The Electronic Marketplace

Behind the markets that consumers regularly see hides a complex warren of transactions and institutions representing the markets where businesses do business with each other. These hidden markets can be arcane, diverse, and often quite inefficient. Most are the legacies of generations of business practices that have become institutionalized, and can range from a formal request for proposal and quote to a walk on a golf course and a handshake.

The automobile industry offers a classic study of this status quo. A typical car has anywhere from four thousand to nine thousand separate parts. Behind every globally recognized automaker—a Ford, a BMW, or a DaimlerChrysler, among others—range a large number of suppliers organized in several hierarchical tiers: from small parts to subassemblies to larger modules.

The automobile supplier hierarchy has a pyramid-like architecture, with the automaker at the top. Each tier of suppliers sells to the tier just above it, with little visibility or access beyond that immediate connection. The automakers are at the top of the pyramid. As a result, demand-side information takes a while to trickle down. Equally important, the pricing between businesses includes multiple layers of markups. These facets of a pyramid-like architecture create inefficiency in the allocation of resources, limited communication across multiple tiers, and inefficient cost structures for the automakers. Any attempt to reconfigure the process to reduce costs would run into the barriers set up by this multilevel, opaque pricing structure.

There has been a growing awareness that the Internet could act as an excellent medium to address many of these issues by replacing the somewhat inefficient status quo with synthetic, electronic markets. Such markets would shift all the diverse supplier transactions to a unified online platform. The pricing and allocation of contracts would be done through auctions to ensure unrestricted competition, thus helping simulate a highly transparent and efficient market. Unlike the status quo, with rules developed through a trial-and-error process of historical evolution, synthetic markets could, in principle, be designed for efficiency. In other words, the *market* itself would be the innovation.

As this idea started taking shape, so did the widespread enthusiasm for the new endgame it envisioned. The size estimates of such markets grew as if in an auction among industry forecasters. Forrester put the value at $2.7 trillion by 2004; the Yankee Group nudged that figure up to $2.78 trillion; the Gartner Group cast its net worldwide and came up with $7.3 trillion.[4] The auto industry electronic market was itself expected to be worth $250 billion annually.

We must keep this dramatic buildup in mind to put the strategic situation in context. A key contributor to the enthusiasm for such markets was a highly publicized big bet by the Big Three automakers: GM, Ford, and DaimlerChrysler. They announced a synthetic marketplace, named for "Cooperation, Vision, Integration"—Covisint—a gigantic, eBay-like auction and exchange platform for businesses in the automobile industry's value system. The system would also promote a high degree of transparency beyond the pricing process itself. Both automakers and their multiple tiers of suppliers could "meet" on Covisint's Web site and conduct real-time conferences on design and engineering issues while working interactively on three-dimensional images of the automobile or its parts. The payoff? The automakers expected that Covisint could shave at least 10 percent off the cost of designing and manufacturing an automobile—a savings that could be shared by all.

The move was a big bet—an irreversible commitment—in many ways. First and foremost, its cocreators were historically bitter industry rivals. "This is an unnatural act, spending so much time with someone from Ford," GM's Harold Kutner was quoted as saying. DaimlerChrysler had other ongoing organizational priorities such as the postmerger integration of Daimler-Benz and Chrysler. This cooperative oddity would disrupt the long-established tradition of head-to-head competition among Detroit's Big Three.

Second, the highly publicized announcement of Covisint meant that these industry competitors were taking on several key groups, whose support was critical to their own viability: the Federal Trade Commission, the labor unions, and the supplier community. None of these other players would relish the prospect of cooperation among the automakers, which would significantly weaken their respective abilities to negotiate.

Third, by declaring a commitment to switch to a more efficient market for their supplies, the automakers were creating expectations of lower prices among consumers. A danger here, of course, is that interest in a transparent market could be extended to the demand side as well. In this scenario, consumers would soon come to expect to be placing orders for customized, transparently priced automobiles online, thereby fundamentally altering the market dynamics.

Fourth, the structure of Covisint itself represented a deep commitment: It was not set up as a small experiment. The founders had committed money, personnel, and prestige to help establish a stand-alone entity. They had done so with no real role models to follow or successful precedents in other industries to emulate. Covisint was meant to be the role model for others.

As an entity, Covisint would be costly to dismantle; a Pandora's box had been opened. This mutual collaboration of several dominant automakers meant that they were tying their hands by foregoing the flexibility of independent, unilateral action.

What led to such a bold commitment? Clearly, the universally bullish forecasts of that time about the future growth of such business-to-business markets played a role. Even so, the magnitude of the bet, its break with the tradition of

competitiveness among automakers, and its early timing suggests that some aspects of the strategic situation facing the
auto industry made the big-bet approach preferable to a more
deliberative, incremental alternative.

Considering the criteria in the diagnostic framework just
presented, the situation in auto industry rated "high" on all
counts and would provide a rationale for placing a big bet.

Motivation to Disrupt the Status Quo

The motivation to change was high. The tiered hierarchy of
the automobile supply chain meant that tier-one suppliers
dealt with tier-two suppliers, which in turn dealt with tier-
three suppliers. The automakers dealt only with tier one. With
multiple layers of markups as each tier negotiated sourcing
contracts with the tier below it, the system allowed little visibility on the contractual details one level below. This added in-
flexibility to the automakers' cost structures. The layers of
markup mattered: Raw materials and parts account for approximately 45 percent of a car's costs. The technology promised
by Internet connectivity appeared, on paper, to cut at least 10
percent of these costs—which itself would strongly motivate
an automaker to establish such a system. Added to these real
costs were the opportunity costs of poor transmission of information through the system. Fixing this information problem
had the potential to create entirely new value propositions,
such as the opportunity to offer made-to-order cars à la Dell
Computer's model for PCs. These motivations contributed to
the case for making a commitment, since the economic benefits
would be so compelling.

Potential for Proprietary Pioneering Benefits

The score on this criterion was expected to be medium to
high. Covisint came before several other major industry con-
sortium exchanges. Its creators recognized at the outset that
there would be a learning curve in establishing a marketplace

such as this with no precedent. Because of its early start, the exchange would have an opportunity to make mistakes, discover the execution challenges, and find ways to integrate the learning back into its development process.

Indeed, there were many execution failures and inner conflicts among Covisint's partners. Making rapid changes in processes and technologies that have been evolving since the early industrial age inevitably creates innumerable difficulties. But there was much learning value. The most compelling benefits of the learning afforded by the early experiments went to those who actually lived through them.

It took Covisint time to overcome several of its early challenges, but it had more time than its rivals to learn and recover. The entire business-to-business synthetic markets idea seemed on the verge of shutting down in other industry sectors. Covisint had done $33 billion worth of transactions by the first half of 2001, and was ranked number five in *InfoWorld*'s list of one hundred companies recognized for the creative use of technology for increasing efficiency and generating new revenue streams. Clearly, there was value to being early in this game.[5]

Need to Create a New Network
Versus Using a Preexisting One

On this, too, the situation scored high. The industry status quo was an entrenched set of legacy practices. The system also needed scale to generate liquidity and lower per-unit transactions costs. In other words, a sufficiently large network of buyers and suppliers was needed up front.

If Covisint were to become the norm by which the auto industry would make its procurements and otherwise collaborate, then the industry would have to make a large up-front investment. It would need to invest in learning the use of a new system, agreements and connectivity among the various suppliers, sharing of data among traditional competitors, and hiring of skilled personnel well versed in Covisint software. Once the investments were made, and other suppliers and procurers were similarly invested, the economics of the new system could be very compelling.

Before Covisint, a network connecting the suppliers and the automaker in a nonhierarchical way simply did not exist. Participants would be inclined to join the network only if they believed that such a network were inevitable and that it would be in their interests not to be left out. A big, collaborative bet among major automakers would be a natural way to establish such a network—and the perception of importance of such a network—in a short period.

Signaling Value

There was also high potential for signaling. Covisint would play a major role in mobilizing wide adoption of the system. The creators of the exchange had sent a credible signal of their commitment, particularly by setting it up as a joint venture among industry competitors. This approach also made it costly to back out, which in turn sent a strong message to the others in the industry about their determination to conduct business primarily on this platform once all the start-up issues had been dealt with.

An investment, especially of a company's reputation, usually signals that it is serious about the endgame it wants to create, is confident about its being realized, and is eager to send a message to other players that they should believe the same. The value of the signal is clear: The more participants that believe in this platform, the more liquid, competitive, and attractive the exchange is, and the more likely it is to create a new, self-reinforcing equilibrium. A big bet is a necessary part of the message: "We have confidence in this market, and so should you. You should believe in our confidence by considering our bold commitment to it."

Barriers to Creating Limited Tests

Covisint scored high on this criterion. A market relies on the volume of transactions and participants for its viability and efficiency. For Covisint, a limited, low-risk pilot would capture few of the benefits—and mimic few of the characteristics—of an appropriately scaled, liquid market. Thus, a certain threshold level of commitment would be necessary.

Leverage Across the Adopter Network

The auto industry's strategic situation would score high on this count as well. The primary players along the critical path of this venture were the various tiers of auto industry suppliers, as well as the partners in Covisint. To the extent that the purpose of the entity is to enforce cooperation, there are obvious mechanisms for the partners to influence one another—at least among the automakers. The pyramid structure of the supply chain would also spread the leverage to the suppliers. The automakers sit on top of the pyramid; their direct line of influence is to the tier-one suppliers, which in turn influence the tier-two suppliers, and so on. Each tier would act as a channel of influence on the next.

There is also a focal-point effect in the formation of a collaborative entity with bold commitments from its founders. The high-profile nature of the announcement and its joint endorsement by the three biggest automakers in the United States helped guarantee that suppliers would sign up.

Finally, for proof that Covisint's founders' leverage would be perceived as high, we need to look no further than the antitrust investigations into Covisint by the Federal Trade Commission in the United States and the Bundeskartellamt in Germany. From each regulator's point of view, Covisint ran the risk of being used as a collusive mechanism, which would give unfair negotiating power to the automakers.

Such leverage would give the founders greater confidence in making the early big bets. They would be justified in the anticipation that they would be in a better position to shape the choices of the other players to steer toward their intended endgame.

RESERVING OPTIONS

In situations that score low on the preceding criteria, a big bet may not be ideal. Instead, you may prudently defer the decision to a point later in the course of a campaign, when more information is available. Reserving the option to act in the future requires that you put some thought into the *triggers* — events that would suggest if the desired endgame has become more or less attractive and attainable based on new data. You may need to plan to implement different kinds of actions after the triggering event. These might include scaling up or scaling down the degree of investment or the speed with which you pursue the endgame, exiting the market, creating another option to defer the decision even further, or modifying the path on which you have begun in some other way.

Several aspects of such triggering events are useful to keep in mind. First, you would want to put in place early indicator systems to anticipate them. Examples of such events are the adoption of the innovation or related products by key market segments, or particular choices by key industry players.

A second element of such contingency-driven plans is that the triggers ought to be limited to a small number. In the absence of such prioritization, the planning becomes too complex, and the systems needed for early warnings too expensive. Also, to the extent that the current action is meant to establish a platform that positions you to take future action, lack of participation limits your ability to be prepared. No platform can be infinitely flexible. Finally, simplicity is important in the communication of the vision to others. All of these are important facets to the innovator's challenge in a networked market, where many players' choices must be coordinated.

Third, if there are a certain number of plausible alternatives to the targeted endgame, you should attempt to identify a trigger for each one. If you lack enough information at the outset to make such distinctions, you should be on the lookout continually as the campaign proceeds.

Finally, in light of these observations, it is useful to ensure that the plausible alternatives under consideration be kept to a small, manageable number. This requires discipline in the process of qualifying endgames at the start of the campaign.

New Applications Software

Although Microsoft's dominance of the software industry is unquestioned, the company rarely takes the lead in introducing innovations in new applications. Instead, it often moves to co-opt the bets of other industry players. In other words, it waits for a new product to be introduced and pass a threshold whereby one of two outcomes becomes likely: Either there is a high-potential new business opportunity for Microsoft, or there is a threat to an existing profitable Microsoft product. At this point, it enters the fray. As history has shown, it enters in a big way. Microsoft's pattern has repeatedly been to defer commitment and reserve the option to co-opt early movers with a decisive bet later.[6]

This commitment approach has been honed over generations of new applications at Microsoft, beginning with its co-optation of the "killer app" that helped bring the PC into wider circulation in the early 1980s. The application was VisiCalc, which ultimately evolved into Lotus's spreadsheet application Lotus 1-2-3.

Microsoft, whose original focus was on the operating system for the PC, decided to monitor the development and adoption of the application that truly fueled the PC's wide adoption.

Only then would it create its own version of the application, under the leadership of Charles Simonyi, formerly of Xerox PARC and an expert on spreadsheet programming. When a version of Microsoft Excel for the Macintosh appeared in 1985, Microsoft had an opportunity to learn from actual usage and feed the learning back into the development process. By 1987, a version for the PC was available. By 1988, Excel was given a further boost with the proliferation of Windows, the user-friendly front end to DOS. Excel subsequently came bundled with Microsoft's Office package, creating a severe competitive disadvantage for Lotus 1-2-3. By 1991, Excel had passed Lotus 1-2-3 in sales and, ten years later, was virtually the only spreadsheet application in existence.

These were the beginnings of a commitment strategy for Microsoft that persisted even as it grew into the predominant player in the industry. Many times, it deferred its bet until some other player had established an initial threshold of proof: The Windows concept followed the innovations in the Apple Macintosh interface; Internet Explorer followed Netscape's Navigator; ActiveX followed Java, originally championed by Sun Microsystems; Windows CE pursued opportunities demonstrated by the success of the Palm Pilot operating system; the MSN portal followed the Internet pioneers Yahoo! and AOL; Windows Media Player was a distant laggard behind Real-Networks; the Xbox game console followed the pioneering PlayStation from Sony. The list is long and covers virtually all the major opportunities for innovation that Microsoft has pursued over the years.

To review this deferred commitment strategy in light of the preceding criteria, consider its entry into the area of Web services, for which MSN was expected to provide a platform. Again, at the time of its entry decision, a new paradigm was on the horizon: a world in which software is no longer purchased and installed on a PC but is instead accessed over the Internet as a service, much like cable TV.

The pioneering players in the field were Hewlett-Packard (HP) and the old NC cabal: Oracle, IBM, and Sun Microsystems. Predictably, several start-ups, BowStreet and WebMethods, were also on the leading edge of this movement. Most of these initiatives, while appealing in principle, were yet to take off—HP's pioneering e-Speak project among them. Microsoft was not a player, but it had contingency plans in place. It was also monitoring developments.

Despite the many capable companies entering this arena, the previously discussed challenges of coordinating a fragmented system of decision makers become evident as one considers the potential for Web services. Since the critical information needed to complete the users' service experience resides on the servers of many different players, the problem of breaking out of an existing equilibrium and reestablishing a new one was already looming on the horizon. Coordinating standards was a major obstacle from the software programming perspective. The situation was rich with the possibility of multiple plausible alternatives to an endgame in which this innovation would be successful.

Several early triggers suggested that Web services would be widely enabled and supported. A once obscure technology, Extensible Markup Language (XML), was emerging as a standard that could hold multiple software tools together. Influential technology evangelists were bandying about stories of compelling applications. In addition, simpler versions of Web services provided by major portals such as Yahoo! and Lycos e-mail and personal calendar accounts offered some early learning experience.

Finally, after certain thresholds of proof—the triggers—had been passed, Microsoft made its entry in June 2000. It announced its Next Generation Windows Services (NGWS) and a new strategy for enabling Windows for a Web-based environment, dubbed Microsoft.Net. Since then, in a little more than a year, Microsoft raced ahead of the others to become one of the principal leaders in the definition of industry standards. Once again, Microsoft had come from behind to co-opt an initiative.

Microsoft's strategic situation scored low on the various criteria discussed in the following sections. The low scores help explain the company's deferred-commitment approach.

Motivation to Disrupt Status Quo

The score on this criterion would be low. Microsoft is a highly successful incumbent in the traditional paradigm in which software is purchased on a onetime basis and installed on the PC for its stand-alone use by consumers. New versions of the software can be purchased and installed in a similar manner. Microsoft incurs a significant amount of risk in actively promoting a migration away from this status quo, which is very profitable in the short term.

The current paradigm, however, might not continue to retain its value. Competing approaches to the traditional model are constantly being investigated by a variety of players. In particular, a subscription-based model of software acquisition looks appealing in a networked environment. In this model, the PC is regarded simply as an access point to a wider set of resources on a network. For this reason, even though it may not be advantageous for a player in Microsoft's situation to proactively disrupt the status quo, it has a strong incentive to scan the horizon for emerging alternatives that can create a new endgame—and to develop its own position in case one such alternative shows signs of taking hold.

Potential for Proprietary Pioneering Benefits

The score on this criterion is also close to low. With virtually every software innovation, there is a "canary" that bears the initial risk of development and has the strong motivation to pioneer a change away from status quo. The canary could be an established competitor, such as Sun Microsystems, motivated by a desire to bypass Microsoft's dominance, or a start-up with a new application or a breakthrough approach. It is clear that only a few such efforts will eventually cross the threshold of plausibility.

Microsoft keeps itself informed of the developments and staffs project teams ready to co-opt competitor products as critical thresholds are close to being crossed. In several instances, it has made preemptive investments in several canaries to give itself the right to participate in an opportunity if one were to emerge, without making a large up-front commitment to it. In all its successful attempts at co-optation, Microsoft has demonstrated that a pioneer's benefits can be co-opted by a player with the capabilities to adapt the technology once it has been proven to work and then scale up rapidly.

Need to Create a New Network Versus Using a Preexisting One

The score on this criterion is low as well. Software is costly to develop initially, but once a market-ready version is created, the ability to distribute it and establish a scalable business depends on access to a network of relationships and partnerships in marketing and sales and product development. If you do not have these networks, the incremental costs of scaling up are very high. If you do have them, the incremental costs can be quite low since software products can be replicated with little additional expenditure. Microsoft has one of the most powerful networks of relationships of any player in the industry.

Microsoft can rely on its preexisting, extensive network to gain huge advantages in scaling up an innovation pioneered by others. Its early development of Windows and subsequent applications relied heavily on a wide network of partner developers. Its deals with Internet service providers, myriad Web sites, and newspapers, as well as its customer network accessible through its 90-percent-plus share of the PC operating system market, were instrumental in the eventual success of Internet Explorer over the pioneering Navigator. This act was repeated in its launch of Windows XP's media technology and formats with more than 150 partners cutting across the information and the entertainment industries. The same can be plausibly expected of its future initiatives.

Signaling Value

There is low signal value in Microsoft's making early investments in emerging software innovations. With its predominant position in the status quo, the company would produce very little *new* information value by making a large investment in promoting an alternative. Even though any significant investment on Microsoft's part would be a widely read message and would be taken very seriously, the default expectation of most market players would be that Microsoft's intent would be the preservation of the status quo. Pioneering the development of an alternative that displaces the status quo in a very visible way would only serve to confuse the rest of the market.

Barriers to Creating Limited Tests

The score on this criterion is low. The nature of software development is such that testing is not only feasible, but also standard practice. Early versions are released to a limited group of users, and market reactions can be evaluated even within such a limited context. In addition, the availability of earlier generations of products—possibly created by others—provides an alternate channel for testing without the company having to make a commitment of significant scale.

Leverage Across the Adopter Network

Surprisingly, Microsoft's score on this criterion is also fairly low, despite its formidable market presence. On the surface, Microsoft would seemingly command an extraordinary amount of influence, even in a highly fragmented decision system. When it comes to introducing new products, however, its leverage to effect change is actually quite limited. The reasons are twofold: First, Microsoft's own motivation is to devote resources and encourage players interested in preserving the status quo. Second, many players on the first stages of the critical path—that is, the early adopters of new applications and the independent developers—are generally motivated to bypass the Microsoft-centric paradigm.

The programming community that acts as the leading edge of developing and bringing software innovations to market has been among the most dedicated in championing alternatives to Microsoft products. This was the case with, say, the development of Java and Linux. Likewise, the early adopters of new Web services are likely to be those looking for alternatives to the traditional PC-centric software purchase model.

Again, with such a bottleneck in mind, Microsoft will wisely let another player with less invested in the status quo test if the innovation is likely to be accepted by early adopters. Once this threshold is close to being passed, Microsoft can step in and lend the ability to scale up the proposition to cover the wider network.

BUYING INSURANCE

The polar ends of commitment choices under uncertainty are to move now and to reserve an option to move later. High scores along the criteria in the framework suggest moving now; low scores suggest reserving the option to move later. There is a third approach. If a situation scores high on the first three criteria but not on the rest, there may be a compelling case for moving early with a relatively sizable and inflexible commitment, while finding ways to reduce the downside risks of making preemptive investments. If the first three criteria tend toward a low score, the case for reserving options becomes stronger.

In the following illustration, an innovator does not have enough levers to narrow the range of the potential outcomes that would follow its initial choice, although it has compelling reasons for moving preemptively. In such circumstances, the innovator must buy insurance. It does so by making the bet and investing in other initiatives that offer a lower bound on the ultimate outcome, no matter which endgame is realized. The purpose of buying insurance, of course, is to minimize the difference in the impact under different plausible endgames. At the extreme, with insurance, even the worst-case scenario should provide some minimum payoff.

What considerations prevent the automatic purchase of an insurance policy? The main deterrent is that it is an expensive, up-front investment. With any form of insurance, you must pay a "premium"—that is, you need to overinvest relative to the investments that would have proven sufficient in the absence of uncertainty.

Networked Entertainment

Although its first product was a rice cooker, Sony is a name virtually synonymous today with entertainment. Whether one speaks of music, movies, games, television, or video, Sony's reach is across the board. Its name appears repeatedly across the value chain: It produces and owns the rights to content, in both music and video, and is one of the world's leading brands in electronics, with TV sets, music players, game consoles, and recording devices in households around the world.

Sony's environment has, however, been changing. The delivery of entertainment has increasingly been intersecting with developments in networking technologies. This has begun to shift the way consumers choose to be entertained, as well as the ways in which content is produced, stored, and delivered to them. According to common wisdom in the entertainment business, it is only a matter of time for the collision between traditional entertainment—Sony's forte—and networked entertainment. Interactive games online, movies on demand, the exchange of music over the Internet are all just over the horizon. In the meantime, the electronics hardware business, Sony's bread and butter, has been experiencing declining margins.

In 1995, during this period of heightened anticipation, Sony got a new leader, Nobuyuki Idei. Idei came into the role with a commitment to placing the company at the center of this innovative collision of entertainment and networking. Idei's declaration removed any doubt about his intentions: "We are bringing entertainment into the network era."[7]

Idei's vision was founded on a flagship product designed to do just that: the forthcoming generation of Sony's popular PlayStation game console. It would be, in Idei's words, "a challenge to Intel and Microsoft." The product would have stand-alone playing capability, could double up as a DVD player, and could be used as an Internet access device. The only trouble, of course, was that the core audience for the product—no matter how popular it was—was still young adults and preteens. The concern was that the product could remain stuck in its original niche as a stand-alone game console. Although Sony was fully committed to making the collision happen, such a challenge to the likes of Intel and Microsoft with a specialized device presented plenty of risks. Entertainment and networking might come together, in other ways.

Sony's approach amounted to a strategy of buying insurance. Consider the target consumer, the individual in a home environment looking for entertainment options delivered over a network. Sony's campaign effectively meant studying the various points of entry of network-borne entertainment into the home and then establishing a significant position at each entry point. These positions each represented large investments. In this sense, they represented more than a reservation of options; they constituted significant hard-to-reverse bets in their own right.

One such entry point into the home was the TV set, a natural place for Sony to start. Already a leading manufacturer of TV sets, Sony now needed to expand its role and to position itself at the link between the TV and the network. Sony launched a broad-based play with a 5 percent investment in General Instruments, the largest set-top box maker; an 11 percent stake in DirecTV, the leading digital satellite system; and an agreement to manufacture and market Internet terminal devices with WebTV, the leading player attempting to transform the TV into the primary Internet access appliance in the home. For added protection, Sony went on to sign agreements with Spyglass for browser software and invested in developing an operating system, Aperios, which could be used in multiple settings, ranging from set-top boxes to game consoles.

Elsewhere in the home, Intel and Microsoft's favorite device, the PC, was still eclipsing the TV as the primary point of consumer access to interactive, network-based content. Sony's presence in the PC industry had historically been minimal—in low-margin cathode-ray-tube PC monitors. As part of its new mandate, Sony made a major investment in a new line of ultrathin laptop PCs with a distinctive design bound to attract notice if the PC were to morph someday into an entertainment appliance. The Vaio group that produced the PCs also invested in many audiovisual technologies, such as digital video recording, in preparation for a world of networked entertainment.

Having dealt with the obvious suspects, Sony was still not satisfied that it had covered all bases. Where else could there be an entry point? It was becoming clear that mobile devices would become a significant medium for receiving entertainment from a network. Sony's home base, Japan, was leading the world in innovative uses of the wireless phone for telecommunications and entertainment. A service called i-Mode was taking off like a rocket. Predictably, Sony went into Internet-ready, wireless handsets as well, and over the years, it inked deals with a disparate group of competing players, such as

Ericsson and Nokia. It invested in other mobile devices like network-enabled digital music players, and cameras.

You might think that all this coverage would have provided Sony some assurance that, no matter how the network brought entertainment into the home, Sony would be there at the entry point. No matter whether consumers would choose a "lean back" mode with a TV set or a "lean forward" mode with a PC or a "get up and walk about" mode with a wireless device, the company had invested in them all. But it was still not satisfied. What about the interworking of all these different modes? What if the true value lay in the interconnection — the home network?

Sony's response to this remaining piece of uncertainty was to invest in the home-networking domain as well. It co-founded a home-networking platform, HAVi, with several other electronics heavyweights. HAVi would set a standard and promote an interface, i.Link, to connect *all* networked devices in the home, regardless of whether they were for entertainment or other purposes.

But wait! There's more! All this coverage was only in a single layer of the networked entertainment value system, the point or device of access to the network. Surely, the real leverage might reside in other parts of the system. In keeping with the insurance mind-set, Sony made bets in several of these other parts as well. These included the online music exchange pressplay mentioned earlier, which was sponsored by its music subsidiary in collaboration with Vivendi Universal; a consumer-entertainment-oriented Web site in collaboration with Yahoo!; and an agreement to develop a broadband network and browser jointly with AOL Time Warner.

All in all, in its virtually end-to-end coverage of the various points of connectivity of entertainment devices to a network, Sony was clearly overinvested. Given the inherent advantages of Intel and Microsoft in PC-centric, lean-forward devices and Sony's historical preference for the TV-centric, lean-back, alternatives, it would have been natural for it to stick to its power play. Sony's insurance scheme, however, would ensure that it would be a player, no matter which endgame were realized.

Like Microsoft, an industry leader like Sony could understandably have made a big, decisive bet and focused its spending. Why, despite Idei's strong declarations, did it choose to take the insurance route and spread its resources so broadly? Some analysts have suggested that Sony may have gone overboard in its desire to cover all bases, potentially leading to a massive organizational and strategic challenge of managing such a vast portfolio.[8]

Unlike Microsoft's wait-and-learn approach, Sony's portfolio took the form of relatively irreversible bets. Why? The framework suggests that Sony did not have enough confidence in a particular endgame to bet on a focused path, but, unlike Microsoft, could not afford to defer its bets.

Motivation to Disrupt the Status Quo

Sony's rating on this criterion would be high. With the oncoming advance of broadband applications, it was quite apparent to Sony's more forward-looking leaders that, if the company did not take steps of its own, the collision of entertainment and networking would take place without Sony's having a seat at the table. Multiple moves in play, particularly on the technology development front, pointed toward the inevitability of this collision. In addition, several powerful competitors, such as Microsoft and AOL Time Warner, were closing in on that space and, by most measures, were already ahead. As a result, it was reasonable for Sony to expect that value would migrate away from its core business.

The status quo for Sony was also becoming unattractive for its own structural reasons. Sony's strength was in hardware electronics, where margins were shrinking. It needed to move its business into an access, service, or software model, with higher margins and recurring revenue streams. For all these reasons, by the mid-1990s the company was quite highly motivated to disrupt the status quo.

Potential for Proprietary Pioneering Benefits

The situation would rate high on this criterion. Unfortunately for Sony, the canaries in this particular innovation would have been none other than Microsoft or AOL Time Warner. By the time Sony would have learned from the data of risks and the most plausible endgame, it would have been too late to mobilize its forces. These canaries, after all, being birds of a very different feather, would have the power and incumbency position in networked markets to make it difficult for a relative newcomer, even one with Sony's reputation and resources. Moreover, there was much to be gained from being a pioneer and gaining early knowledge of how the convergence of entertainment and networking was evolving.

Further, appliances such as a network-enabled TV or home networking have a high switching cost. Once a consumer has learned a system, especially one that involves the kind of complexity associated with networked products, it is hard to displace an early mover. In a home environment, the product refresh cycle is longer than in corporate environments. This confers additional benefits to a pioneer.

Need to Establish a New Network
Versus Using a Preexisting One

The score on this criterion would also be high. As observed earlier, the prime competitors to Sony were players such as Microsoft and AOL. They would be potential beneficiaries of their own preexisting networks and relationships. Their powerful distribution and partnering capabilities implied that Sony would have to establish a network of its own or form an alliance with an incumbent player. This, in turn, created a need to move early and make a substantial investment in order to establish scale effects.

Signaling Value

Sony's situation would rate a medium on this front. It was important for Sony to send a message to the incumbents in the relevant information industries that it was ready to play in their territory and leverage its existing connections with consumers. Even if this meant a significant overinvestment in alternative paths of entry, the value of the signal was high. It would give Sony access to partners and perhaps even potential competitors that Sony could join hands with. Thus, Sony announced an agreement with AOL Time Warner, ordinarily one of its primary competitors, to codevelop a broadband network, a browser, and other means of enabling the collision of networking and entertainment.

Idei's early declarations had sent the message of talking the talk. Early investments provided the real signal that the company was prepared to back it up by walking the proverbial walk as well. The overall signal value may, however, have been diffused by the sheer breadth of networked entertainment and by the presence of Sony's brand name in multiple places in the entertainment value chain. There was no single point of focus that would stand out as a clear signal of its intent. In fact, given the extent of its initial reach, it would have a difficult time creating a clearly readable signal.

Barriers to Creating Limited Tests

Sony's situation would score medium to low on this criterion. On the one hand, consumers' evolving behavior toward how they choose to be entertained can be, and is, tested through pilots and experiments and even in simulated experiences in labs. Even so, network effects and cultural shifts may make such tests imperfectly predictive of market reaction in a scaled-up, realistic setting. Several of these "softer" and quirkier aspects of consumer adoption behavior with regard to entertainment make them somewhat more challenging to simulate.

Moreover, the evolving nature of the network's penetration into the home itself further undermined the validity of the tests. This is because the adoption of network-based services in the home could involve multiple family members in a decision about things other than entertainment—a situation hard to replicate through simulation.

Indeed, experiences in one region do not easily translate into experiences in others, for a variety of cultural, technological, and economic reasons. For example, although toys and games have traveled well from Japan to other parts of the world, the use of messaging by cell phone has not. Online gaming, hugely popular in South Korea, may not necessarily find similar popularity elsewhere. The networking habits in Scandinavian countries have been hard to replicate in other regions.

Leverage Across the Adopter Network

Sony's situation would score low on this criterion. Although it had a recognized consumer products brand name, Sony had limited leverage over the decision-making system in a networked environment. Its hardware and content businesses themselves had not gained the kind of synergy that was hoped for on paper, making it hard for Sony to use its combined might in creating sufficient leverage. The low score on this criterion would constrain Sony's ability to steer toward its desired endgame. Protection from alternative, less favorable outcomes would therefore be necessary, given the demands on Sony to make substantial, irreversible investments up front.

The mixed nature of the scorecard for Sony suggests that it could not afford to fall behind and yet was not in a position to eliminate the substantial uncertainties. To play the game, it simply had to take out insurance.

COMMITMENTS THAT CAN DEFINE THE COMPANY

Innovation is an act of disequilibrium. It is meant to perturb a self-reinforcing status quo. Because the network of affected players can react in many different ways, the outcome is uncertain. And then there is the confounding effect of networking. The interlinkages among the players means that reactions in one part of this system may trigger twisted chains of reactions elsewhere. This, too, produces uncertainty. It is in such a context that an innovator must qualify and commit to a journey toward an endgame.

Many find uncertainty unsettling. Uncertainty in a networked setting may be especially unsettling since it is less visible in the fragmented state of decision making. Nevertheless, given that you cannot eliminate uncertainty, you are better off acknowledging its presence and dealing with it in a suitable manner. This chapter offers a framework for deciding how much to commit to a strategy targeted at one's desired endgame.

The uncertainty that I speak of, however, is *residual*. It is what is left after an innovator has attempted to anticipate the behaviors of the players in a network, based on an analysis of their respective choice factors and the impact each player has on the others. If the strategist understands the choice factors that explain the gap between the endgame and status quo, the uncertainty ought to be reduced to a handful of discrete possibilities rather than an unwieldy and wide continuum.

Still, the commitments required may affect not just the course of an innovation, but the destinies of entire companies. Frequently, it is the commitment to a particular strategic choice with regard to innovation that ends up defining a company. For example, Sony bought an insurance policy that required a broad portfolio of commitments on many fronts spanning the entire organization.

The commitment to a strategic choice defined the protagonist with which we began this chapter. IBM, under Louis Gerstner Jr., made a bet on transforming itself into a largely services- and solutions-oriented business—an innovative divergence from the prevailing conventional wisdom that the company was beyond repair and would have to be broken up.

Similarly, Xerox also took steps to diverge from its legacy. It was quietly steering itself away from both the copying and the printing businesses—decisions that it struggled with earlier. It was preparing for an increased focus on data—its storage and management—rather than on documents. Not ready yet to declare a big bet, Xerox simply chose to reserve an option to commit later in the future. Publicly, its only noticeable change was to reduce, in its advertising copy, the size of the famous Xerox byline: "The Document Company."[9] Only slowly would the market come to realize Xerox's intent to withdraw from the very endgame once invented and engineered by the up-start Haloid Company back in 1959.

Chapter Eight

BEWARE OF LOUD NOISES

You know what's the loudest noise in the world, man?
The loudest noise in the world is silence.

—Thelonious Monk, jazz pianist and composer

CHARLES DARWIN'S COUSIN Francis Galton had an evocative metaphor for organisms as objects waiting to being struck by the forces of natural selection. The paleontologist Stephen Jay Gould, in extending the metaphor, describes the objects as billiard balls with natural selection as the cue. There was one exception. Galton's ball was really a polyhedron—with many flat surfaces.[1] Such a ball would have two interesting properties. It is stable in the status quo because it rests on one of its surfaces, and when hit by the cue, it goes in one of a small number of directions within a bounded range.

The Galton-Gould evolutionary pool table tells our story as well. The market is the polyhedron-shaped ball. Innovation is the cue that brings about disequilibrium. When innovation arrives on the scene, an equilibrium is in place. Here things already work in a status quo; maybe they work clumsily or in inefficient ways. A pattern of behaviors and a market protocol may have congealed around this status quo. It is this situation

181

of rest—which may be viewed as gridlock by some and as a stable market by others—that innovations in a connected world must pry apart.

That, however, is only half the story. At the other end, innovations must create a new situation in which different behaviors become the norm so that once the industry has adjusted and the dust has settled, the innovation is part of a new status quo. The tangled nature of an interconnected market assures us that once the status quo is disturbed, a new equilibrium will form—a new, flat surface of rest in the case of Galton's polyhedron.

This two-part journey to market must follow the other better-documented aspects of the innovation cycle: the eureka moment; the development of technology to give life to an idea; and the creation of an organization to produce and commercialize the innovation. My emphasis has been on the issues that must be dealt with once these stages have passed—that is, on innovation's endgame.

The purpose of this final chapter is three-fold. The first is to recap some of the key points made in earlier chapters. The second is to offer an extension of the framework developed here and relate it to two alternative perspectives on the strategy of innovation and new market entry. The third is to close with a reflection on the overall context for our discussion, the connected world, and its broader implications for both the innovator and the strategist.

RECAP: KEY POINTS

This book has covered several topics related to matching up innovations to markets in the context of a connected world. Here are some of the main ideas from the preceding discussions. These ideas will be relevant both for interpretation and anticipation, as well as for taking action:

- Innovators and their champions tend to set their sights on the social benefits of innovation. Decisions in a market

setting are made at the level of the individual. Therefore, for an innovation to make headway in the market,
an innovator must examine its benefits in a limited, private context. This context is particularly constrained
when individuals are interconnected. Simply dividing
the social benefit by the number of individuals in society will not provide an answer.

- Technology almost always deceives us into thinking
  that we are going to progress further than the fragmented reality of the market will allow us. This dispar-
  ity has several effects. First, we must keep in mind
  some rule of thumb—a demi-Moore's Law for the market in question—that tempers the technologist's opti-
  mistic predictions when setting expectations for
  technology's impact.

    Second, we should expect the past to linger on, with
  the earlier behaviors having congealed into equilibrium.
  Even when the future equilibrium takes shape, it will bear
  more resemblance to its predecessor than we would have
  expected. Paul Duguid, in an incisive commentary on the
  stubbornness of the past, cites the example of the hinged
  door, a vivid illustration of this point.[2] Since the 1930s, our
  visions—in sci-fi movies, on *Star Trek*, and in our imagina-
  tions—of the doors of future have been hingeless. Our future is usually one of sliding doors. Yet the hinge has hung
  on and shows no signs of coming off. It has even tran-
  scended doors. We see it daily in flip-open cell phones,
  PDAs, and laptops—and other door-inspired designs.
  The many mutually reinforcing aspects of the equilibrium
  do not all unravel in a single cycle of change.

- Our discussion on strategy highlighted four aspects of
  building a campaign designed to bring innovation into
  the markets of a connected world: (1) qualifying the
  endgame and, in the process, choosing between several
  strategic options at the outset; (2) orchestrating the

changes necessary across the network of players through a mechanism that propagates the innovator's selective interventions into the wider network; (3) actively managing interactions with the critical agents that will pass on the innovation's influence; and (4) making appropriate choices on how to commit to strategies that lead to certain endgames in the face of uncertainty—depending on the situation, one must choose between making a bet, reserving options, and seeking insurance.

- Finally, what makes these considerations distinctive is the networked market context in which the innovations must play. This context presents the innovator with a unique set of challenges and opportunities. Although interconnectivity of such markets is not new, its intensity and central role in practically every sector of modern markets in this information age is without precedent.

EXTENDING THE EQUILIBRIUM FRAMEWORK

The uncertain nature of how innovations originate and their subsequent path to market has led many others to reflect on several implications of managing innovation and entry into new markets. The framework of equilibrium can be extended as a useful integrating mechanism to put these different ideas into perspective. Consider two of the most influential ones.

The Innovator's Dilemma

Clayton Christensen has focused on the inherent difficulty that successful incumbent firms experience when they simultaneously try to become successful innovators in their own industries.[3] He writes about the dilemma that such firms face, whose very success depends on serving their current best customers.

This juxtaposition creates a disincentive to pursue innovations that would disrupt this status quo. Yet, even successful firms recognize that in a competitive world they must innovate to preserve their position of leadership in the next round of play.

Within our framework, one such firm would be caught between trying to be the steward of two distinct equilibria. It would like to continue mining the one that has made it successful. It would also like to unlock the current equilibrium and establish a new one. Unfortunately, the network that the incumbent currently owns is meant to serve its current customers and preserve the status quo equilibrium. Utilizing the network for both purposes would give rise to conflict.

While many interpretations of the innovator's dilemma explore its implications for organization strategy, ours helps turn toward the implications for competitive and market-oriented strategy. The equilibrium interpretation lends some perspective to the competitive asymmetry between the incumbent and an innovator that is a new entrant in the market. The incumbent owns a network because of the access and relationships and products it has in place. Its challenge is to piggyback its innovation onto this network, without creating a conflict with its core business. While the entrant is not conflicted, since its interest lies unambiguously with the new equilibrium, it does have the handicap of having to establish a network from scratch.

Network Effects As Barriers to Entry

Networked markets may play a role in establishing barriers to entry for innovations that challenge incumbents that own a network. W. Brian Arthur and Paul David, among many others, have written about this theory, which had experienced intense scrutiny and exposure particularly during the antitrust proceedings against Microsoft.[4]

Networks have a property that endows them with economies of scale: The benefits of being on the network to any party depends on the size of the network itself. In other words, the wider the network built around your product the greater the value to each member of that network. This situation has the potential to create a barrier to entrants by diminishing individual motivations of consumers to change. Technically, the entrant may have a superior product yet it could still remain locked out of the network.

A framing of such a situation in our framework would be as a status quo equilibrium. This equilibrium could survive despite the presence of a superior alternative because the network effect creates mutually self-reinforcing choices that lock in the status quo. We saw an example of such implicit barriers to entry of information technology in the case of health care discussed in chapter 1.

THE OVERALL CONTEXT: SHOULD WE BE WORRIED ABOUT A CONNECTED WORLD?

Many of those who make it their business to speculate on future innovations speak of even greater interconnectivity ahead. Top innovations to watch, according to the Institute for the Future, involve the tangling of disciplines like bio-interactive materials, combinatorial science, and quantum nucleonics.[5] If these developments come to pass, connectivity will span information technology, materials science, bioscience and energy, among a host of others. If the future follows the futurists, even more interconnection lies ahead.

I have already observed that the connected world can be a rather odd place. Far from perfect, it can produce a web of imperfections. With faster computer processing speeds and wider networks, the processing through market can turn out to be surprisingly slow. A better product may not be a best choice. On net, choices made by individuals connected to one another produce unexpected results when they add up. And it is a world such as this that modern innovators must contend with.

The unexpected nature of the connected world is not entirely a bad thing, though. I began this book on a note of sobriety, with references to the prisoner's dilemma and the cold, rational framework of game theory. I would like to close with a far more uplifting paradigm—which is as far removed as possible from either science or business.

Although the dismal scientists and mathematicians were puzzling over John Nash's beautiful bind or prisoner's dilemmas, unbeknownst to them, children in the 1950s were also being introduced to the paradoxes of the connected world in a very different way. They were reading Benjamin Elkin's new book, *The Loudest Noise in the World*. Its message is one that I find highly germane to the innovator and strategist.

The Loudest Noise in the World is set in the land of Hub-Bub. As the name suggests, it was indeed a noisy land.[6] Its citizens celebrated cacophony: Cars honked their horns louder, people spoke at the top of their voices and clanged their pots and pans, and folks went about their daily business in a very noisy way. In this melee was raised the Prince Hulla-Baloo, who too had a thing about noise. His doting father promised his son and heir anything he wanted for his upcoming birthday. Instead of asking for the equivalent of the latest-generation video-game console for those days (as any reasonable boy would), the prince had loftier needs. He wanted to hear the loudest noise in the world.

Done, said Dad, who promptly dispatched emissaries to the far reaches of the world to coax, cajole, and threaten every human capable of sound to shout *Happy Birthday* at the top of his or her voice at the appointed time on the little brat's birthday. Since this was all before the time of e-mail or CNN or direct marketing, you can imagine that the king had a tough information technology problem to solve in getting the word out. Granted, the world had fewer people then, but, amazingly, not a single denizen of the planet was left out. Of course, everyone simply loved the idea. The more people signed up, the more excited everyone was about hearing the loudest noise in the world. The critical day was eagerly anticipated — in fact, most folks could barely wait.

Of course, Elkin's prince had, unwittingly, created a global network effect — but with just one little snag. If everyone shouts, then no one actually hears the loudest noise in the world — other than the prince, of course. Some time before the momentous day, one individual had a revelation: If instead of joining in the shouting, he were to keep quiet and listen, then he too would get to hear the loudest noise. Since his voice was just one among so many, what would remain would still be the loudest noise in the world. The idea was too brilliant, of course, to keep to himself. The man told his wife, who thought it was swell and decided she would try it herself; surely her lone defection would make no difference. But this was such a good idea that her friend would just die if she told her. So she did. And so on.

You can imagine that such good ideas have a tendency to carry. And before long, from Arkansas to Zaire, someone had heard about this terrific plan from a particularly helpful acquaintance. Faithful readers of earlier chapters of this book will surely recognize a version of the infecting mechanism at work.

The prince's birthday arrived. The air was filled with anticipation. The prince went out onto his balcony to get an earful of the loudest noise in the world. The clock rang on the appointed hour, and it was followed by . . . nothing. A still serenity filled the air. There was, indeed, nothing but the sounds of the birds. Naturally, the prince was shocked and, appropriately, speechless. But then he heard something he had never heard before: the sound of the wind in the leaves, of water, of birds singing. He loved it. It was a joy he had never experienced before. He rushed and told his father that this was indeed the best birthday present he could ever have had. Now, apart from the inhabitants of distant Pacific islands and others who live in such circumstances on a daily basis (who must have gotten a raw deal), the blissful absence of sound was truly an unexpected bonus.

To put this fable in the terminology of this book (diligent readers will have pounced on the answer already): The loudest noise in the world was just not a plausible endgame. The king had, in his benevolence, relied on a fragmented network of individually motivated players to contribute to the birthday present. Shouting at the top of one's voice and missing out on the din would not have been a best choice for anyone, no matter what was expected of the others. Although the final outcome was a surprise, the choices, considered in the narrow, private context in which choices actually get made, were quite unsurprising.

In the last several years, as an even more connected world has come together, we have been promised a "loudest noise" of limitless innovation. There were loud ideas—some even with fitting names such as boo.com. As we know from Elkin's fable or from the contemporary tales from the earlier chapters, we ought not to be surprised by the silence. Loud noises—or even silences, for that matter—depend on whether they arise as best choices from the private perspectives of the players who are affected by them. And, as we have seen in the case of the prince, silence has its virtues.

We may never get the perfect market that delivers the loudest noise or pet food bought over the Internet to our door. Or, as in the case with boo.com, we may never have the opportunity to try haute couture in our pajamas. Thank goodness. Yet, toward the end of the twenty-first century, we will undoubtedly look back at the beginning of this century much as we look back at the beginning of the last one. We will find it remarkable how far we have come. We may, finally, even have sliding doors.

Strategically speaking, market imperfection—in silences or in the many pauses we have encountered—is the mother of innovation. Imperfection gives us reason to innovate, not just

in the product but also in the campaign for getting the innovative product to market. And it is toward this last point that
I hope this book makes a contribution.

Of course, these imperfections will also create uncertainty
at every stage of the game, which justifies an innovator's return. Market imperfection will form the kernel of competitive
asymmetry, the basis for sustaining the returns over time.
Otherwise, the connected world would drive toward equal access to all, where information is spread widely and quickly. In
such a symmetric world, the challenges—and rewards—of
getting an innovation to market would diminish. And the
strategist in every innovating company would be inquiring
into other occupations.

This is why, when all is said and done, this book is not
meant as a dismal message about yet another incarnation of
the prisoner's dilemma. The slow pace of fast change is good
news for the strategic innovator. In fact, it is essential news.

Next time you think about progress, pause. Do you now
hear the sounds of the birds singing?

NOTES

Preface

1. Bhaskar Chakravorti, "Demi-Monde of IT Progress," *Financial Times*, 27 May 1998. As to what Demi Moore had to do with all this, the reader will have to read ahead to chapter 2.

2. Michael E. Porter, *Competitive Strategy: Techniques for Analyzing Industries and Competitors* (New York: Free Press, 1998); Pankaj Ghemawat, *Commitment: The Dynamic of Strategy* (New York: Free Press, 1991); Adam M. Brandenburger and Barry J. Nalebuff, *Co-opetition* (New York: Doubleday, 1997); Geoffrey Moore, *Crossing the Chasm: Marketing and Selling High-Tech Products to Mainstream Customers* (New York: HarperBusiness, 1999); Adrian Slywotsky, David J. Morrison, and Bob Andelman, *The Profit Zone: How Strategic Business Design Will Lead You To Tomorrow's Profits* (New York: Times Books, 1998).

3. Thomas S. Kuhn, *The Structure of Scientific Revolutions* (Chicago: University of Chicago Press, 1996); Everett Rogers, *The Diffusion of Innovations* (New York: Free Press, 1995); James M. Utterback, *Mastering the Dynamics of Innovation* (Boston: Harvard Business School Press, 1994); Carl Shapiro and Hal R. Varian, *Information Rules* (Boston: Harvard Business School Press, 1998); John Seely Brown and Paul Duguid, *The Social Life of Information* (Boston: Harvard Business School Press, 2000); Malcolm Gladwell, *The Tipping Point* (Boston: Little, Brown and Company, 2000); W. Brian Arthur, *Increasing Returns and Path Dependence in the Economy* (Ann Arbor: University of Michigan Press, 1994); Clayton M. Christensen, *The*

Innovator's Dilemma: When New Technologies Cause Great Firms to Fail (Boston: Harvard Business School Press, 1997); Jean Tirole, *The Theory of Industrial Organization* (Cambridge, MA: MIT Press, 1988); Drew Fudenberg and Jean Tirole, *Game Theory* (Cambridge, MA: MIT Press, 1991).

Chapter 1

1. Herbert Hoover, *Popular Science*, 1922, quoted in Merritt Ierley, *Wondrous Contrivances: Technology at the Threshold* (New York: Clarkson Potter Publishers, 2002).

2. "Distributing Music over Telephone Lines," *Telephony Magazine*, 18 December 1909, 699–701.

3. This proposition has been made in many ways and under several names: from Robert Metcalfe, a founder of 3Com and inventor of the Ethernet; to George Gilder, the well-known forecaster on telecommunications and technology; to Matthew from the New Testament ("For to everyone who has will more be given, and he will have abundance, but from him who has not, even what he has will be taken away"); see Wu Jiapei, "Several Issues on the Network Economy and Economic Governance," available online at <http://unpan1.un.org/intradoc/groups/public/documents/un/unpan001373.pdf> (accessed 22 August 2002).

4. As is now well known, few were content with the slowness of the pace. Although boo.com folded and its assets were sold before it could get into any more trouble, WorldCom and Enron became the subjects of investigation for allegedly misleading their investors about the true slowness of the pace they were experiencing.

5. This is a reference to the Academy Award–winning movie *A Beautiful Mind* (Universal Studios and Dreamworks, 2001), based on Sylvia Nasar, *A Beautiful Mind: The Life of Mathematical Genius and Nobel Laureate John Nash* (New York: Touchstone Books, 2001).

6. A paraphrasing of a description by Roger Myerson in "Nash Equilibrium and the History of Economic Theory," *Journal of Economic Literature* 37 (1999): 1067–1082, can be found in David Warsh's article "The Nash Program," *Boston Globe*, 30 December 2001.

7. See the discussion on networks and definitions in Carl Shapiro and Hal Varian, *Information Rules* (Boston: Harvard Business School Press, 1998).

8. Not entirely hypothetical though, having agonized over similar issues with my own eleven-year-old.

9. Such concerns have been raised by several analysts. See Irene Kunii, Cliff Edwards, and Jay Greene "Can Sony Regain the Magic?" *Business Week*, 11 March 2002.

10. In the literature on industrial organization, competition across generations of durable goods is commonly called the Coase conjecture; see Ronald H. Coase, "Durability and Monopoly," *Journal of Law and Economics* 15 (1972): 143–149.

11. Definition adapted from Everett M. Rogers, *The Diffusion of Innovations*, 4th ed. (New York: Free Press, 1995).

12. Personal communication from Monitor Group client on study conducted by Healtheon, 2000.

13. Health-care organizations spend on average 4 percent of their revenue on information technology; for financial services the figure is closer to 10 percent.

14. Cited in Bob Tedeschi, "No Fun for Sisyphus: The Woes of WebMD and Medscape," *New York Times*, 26 October 2000.

15. Joseph A. Schumpeter, *Capitalism, Socialism and Democracy* (New York: HarperCollins, 1984).

16. For more on Kodak's history, see Merritt Ierley, *Wondrous Contrivances: Technology at the Threshold* (New York: Clarkson Potter Publishers, 2002).

17. As in the case of the computers and their applications, technological breakthroughs can play an important role in focusing the efforts of different players acting somewhat independently. The digital camera may have such a focal point in Carver Mead. His company, Foveon, introduced the X3 chip, which could dramatically transform the color resolution quality of digital cameras. And if his track record in semiconductors and microchip design is any indication, Mead's interest in digital imaging may be crucial in further galvanizing the implicit coordination.

18. See Drew Fudenberg and Jean Tirole, *Game Theory* (Cambridge, MA: MIT Press, 1991).

19. For example, see Jean Tirole, *The Theory of Industrial Organization* (Cambridge, MA: MIT Press, 1988), for application to industrial organization; Ghemawat, *Commitment*, Brandenburger and Nalebuff, *Co-opetition*, for application to business strategy; Paul Milgrom, *Auction Theory for Privatization* (Cambridge: Cambridge University Press, 2003), for application to auctions and public policy; Robert Wright, *Non-Zero: The Logic of Human Destiny* (New York: Pantheon Books, 1999), for application to evolution and development of human

cultures; Francis Fukuyama, *The Great Disruption: Human Nature and Reconstitution of Social Order* (New York: Free Press, 1999), for application to social change; John Maynard Smith, *Evolution and the Theory of Games* (Cambridge: Cambridge University Press, 1982), for application to evolutionary biology; Peter Ordeshook, *Game Theory and Political Theory* (Cambridge: Cambridge University Press, 1986), for application to political science; William Poundstone, *Prisoner's Dilemma: John von Neumann, Game Theory and the Puzzle of the Bomb* (New York: Doubleday, 1992), for application to nuclear deterrence.

20. See Anne Marie Chaker, "The Birth of a Cult Sweetener," *Wall Street Journal*, 21 May 2002.

Chapter 2

1. Moore's Law was not meant to be a mathematically precise statement about semiconductor technology. It is an average of two separate, broad predictions. Moore's original 1965 article in *Electronics* magazine predicted that "the complexity [of cheap integrated circuits] has increased at a rate of roughly a factor of two a year. . . . Over the longer term . . . there is no reason to believe [the rate of increase] will not remain constant for at least 10 years." Gordon Moore, "Cramming More Components Onto Integrated Circuits," *Electronics* 38, no. 8 (1965). Indeed, ten years later, at the annual International Electronics Devices meeting of the Institute of Electrical and Electronics Engineers, Moore acknowledged the difficulty of the chipmaking process and revised his predictions down to a rate of doubling every two years. Today, most people give him the benefit of the doubt and are happy to split the difference. See Charles Mann, "The End of Moore's Law?" *Technology Review*, May–June 2000, 42–48.

2. Mann, "The End of Moore's Law?"

3. Productivity is most generally described as the amount of output produced per unit of input. The actual definition could vary depending on the methods and data of empirical studies being used to measure it. Although it isn't everything, Princeton economist Paul Krugman reportedly said that, in the long run, productivity is almost everything. See E. Brynjolfsson and L. Hitt, "Beyond the Productivity Paradox: Computers Are the Catalyst for Bigger Changes," *Communications of the ACM* [Association for Computing Machinery] 41, no. 8 (1998): 49–55.

4. E. Raper, "VisionQuest 2000," cited in *Computer Retail Week*, 9 February 1998.

5. Thomas Nast's famous nineteenth-century cartoon in *Harper's Weekly*, about the notorious New York mayor "Boss" Tweed and his cronies in Tammany Hall, has a caption that asks, "Who took the money?" Tweed and his fellow administrators are depicted standing in a ring, each pointing to the person next to him. One can see a similar "Tweed ring" in the case of the 56K modem. If Thomas Nast were to sketch the 56K ring, he may well ask, "Which standard would you support?" Each participant in the ring would point to the next participant and respond, "Whichever he or she is supporting." I am grateful to the late Richard McKelvey of Caltech for bringing this analogy to my attention.

6. This is no easy task, given that the product needs to be sold simultaneously to multiple players in the circle. Later chapters describe common strategies for solving this simultaneous-adoption problem.

7. During this time, 3Com, the market leader in making "head-end" servers, even merged with U.S. Robotics, the original champion of the X2.

8. Finally, in February 1998, the International Telecommunications Union (ITU) announced a common standard for the 56K modem that officially ended the contest. The union had acted, though belatedly, as a central coordinating authority. The market participants finally had a new focal point around which their choices could converge. "Faster Modem Accord Reached," Online County News (National Association of Counties), 2 March 1998, <http://www.naco.org/pubs/cnews/98-03-02/webwatch.htm> (accessed 14 October 2002). Interestingly, stock in both 3Com and Rockwell rose after the announcement.

9. Robert S. Solow, "We'd Better Watch Out," *New York Times Book Review*, 12 July 1987.

10. See Robert J. Gordon, "Does the 'New Economy' Measure Up to the Great Inventions of the Past?" *Journal of Economic Perspectives* 14 (2000): 4.

11. "Productivity on Stilts," *The Economist*, 10 June 2000.

12. Even the jump to 2.5 percent does not pass Professor Gordon's burden of proof (Gordon, "Does the 'New Economy' Measure Up?"). He argues that once you subtract the productivity improvements in the computing, peripherals, telecoms, and other durables sector and the contribution of the investments in such durables, the underlying structural improvement in productivity in the economy at large has actually decelerated.

13. See W. Brian Arthur, "Is the Information Revolution Dead?" *Business 2.0*, March 2002, <http://www.business20.com/articles/mag/0,1640,37570,FF.html> (accessed 18 December 2002).

14. See Robert Strauss, "You've Got Maelstrom: Dealing with Too Much E-Mail," *New York Times*, 5 July 2001.

15. The e-mail inefficiency is part of a broader family of social dilemmas that many others have discussed outside the context of communications networks. The Nobel laureate Paul Samuelson has written about the "free-rider problem" that arises with broadly shared resources. Similarly, the biologist Garrett Hardin has described the phenomenon in a wider variety of contexts as the "tragedy of the commons." The concerns here are that each subscriber to the resource has an interest in downplaying his or her interest in it in the hope of lowering the tax burden or subscription he or she may be called upon to bear; everybody hopes to free-ride off others under the belief that the unilateral misrepresentation has negligible impact. Since this logic is universally applied, the resource is severely undersupported, to everyone's detriment. A voluminous literature grown out of the recognition of such problems suggests public policy solutions to overcome such inefficiency. See Theodore Groves and John Ledyard, "Incentive Compatibility since 1972" in *Information, Incentives and Economic Mechanisms: Essays in Honor of Leonid Hurwicz*, ed. Theodore Groves, Roy Radner, and Stanley Reiter (Minneapolis: University of Minnesota Press, 1987), for a survey of the early phase of this literature.

16. See Michael Learmonth, "The Best of Enemies," *The Industry Standard*, 11 June 2001.

17. The term is most frequently associated with the ideas in the book of the same name: Robert J. Shiller, *Irrational Exuberance* (Princeton, NJ: Princeton University Press, 2000).

18. Tom Jacobs, "Europe's 3G Debt Hangover," <http://www.fool.com/news/2001/tele010104.htm> (accessed 29 October 2002).

19. See Jamie Earle, "Why 3G Should Fear the Wireless LAN," <http://news.com.com/2010-1075-921563.html> (accessed 29 October 2002).

20. Ronald Coase, "The Nature of the Firm," *Economica* (1937): 4.

21. Clayton Christensen in his work on disruptive technologies observes the potential for such conflict and advises that separate entities may be necessary to go after such innovations. Clayton M. Christensen, *The Innovator's Dilemma: When New Technologies Cause Great Firms to Fail* (Boston: Harvard Business School Press, 1997).

22. David Dranove and Neil Gandal, "The DVD and DIVX

Standard War: Empirical Evidence of Vaporware," working paper CPC01-016, Institute of Business and Economic Research, Competition Policy Center, University of California, Berkeley, CA, 1 November 2000, <http://repositories.cdlib.org/iber/cpc/CPC01-016> (accessed 26 November 2002).

Chapter 3

1. John F. Nash, "Equilibrium Points in N-Person Games," *Proceedings of the National Academy of Sciences* 36 (1950); Nash, "Non-Cooperative Games," *Annals of Mathematics* 54 (1951).

2. Interestingly enough, the labels agreed to settle a price-fixing lawsuit for a $67.3 million payment. The suit was brought by forty-three states against the labels and three retailers, charging that they engaged in advertising practices that kept the prices of CDs artificially high. Lisa M. Bowman, "Labels Pay to Settle Price-Fixing Suit," CNET News.com, 30 September 2002, <http://news.com.com/2100-1023-960183.html> (accessed 26 November 2002).

3. Peter H. Lewis, "Napster Rocks the Web," *New York Times*, 29 June 2001.

4. To see how Napster was further integrated into the MusicNet coalition, see John Borland and Jim Hu, "Napster Signs on to Sell Major Labels' Music," CNET News.com, <http://news.com.com/2100-1023-267840.html?tag=rn> (accessed 29 October 2002).

5. The sites have begun cross-licensing with labels from the opposite coalition. See Lisa Bowman, "MusicNet, Pressplay Closing in on Labels," CNET News.com <http://news.com.com/2100-1023-962179.html?tag=mainstry> (accessed 18 December 2002).

Chapter 4

1. Quoted in Ira Flatow, *They All Laughed* (New York: Harper Perennial, 1993).

2. See Mike Wilson, *The Difference Between God and Larry Ellison: Inside Oracle Corporation* (New York: Morrow, 1997).

3. Larry Ellison, quoted in Mark Hachman, "Larry Ellison, President, CEO, Oracle Corp.," EBN (Electronic Buyers' News) Web site, <http://www.ebnonline.com/hot25/ellison.html> (accessed 26 November 2002).

4. Larry Ellison, speech to the Commonwealth Club of California, 8 March 1996, <http://www.commonwealthclub.org/archive/96/96-03ellison-speech.html> (accessed 29 October 2002).

5. See "Five Companies Work Together Against Microsoft; Novell Among Group Hoping to Topple High-Tech Leader," *Salt Lake Tribune*, 16 November 1997.

6. For details on Adobe history and features, see <http://www.planetpdf.com> and links therein (accessed 29 October 2002).

7. See Peter Schwartz, *The Art of the Long View: Planning for the Future in an Uncertain World* (New York: Wiley, 1997).

8. Based on Monitor Group analyses of the antidepressant-prescribing behavior in the United States, 1998–1999, described in internal communications. Also see David Morrow, "Lusting After Prozac: Drug Makers in Hot Race For a New Market Leader," *New York Times*, 11 October 1998.

9. The difficulty of reasoning back from an endgame is most charmingly demonstrated by the "centipede game" described by Robert Rosenthal, "Games of Perfect Information, Predatory Pricing, and Chain-Store Paradox," *Journal of Economic Theory* 25 (1981). Senior executives rarely reason backward in new situations, although they intuitively apply the principle in situations with which they are familiar in experimental games run in Monitor Group management development sessions. The data was consistent in experiments conducted with executives across multiple industries: high technology, health care, consumer products, and financial services.

Chapter 5

1. Cited in Thomas Friedman, "Reeling but Ready," *New York Times*, 28 April 2002.

2. David Henry, "Mergers: Why Most Big Deals Don't Pay Off," *BusinessWeek*, 14 October 2002.

3. Malcolm Gladwell, *The Tipping Point* (Boston: Little, Brown and Company, 2000).

4. See <http://www.nd.edu/~networks/linked/newfile9.htm> (accessed 29 October 2002), and the related book by Albert-Lasso Barabasi, *Linked: The New Science of Networks* (Cambridge, MA: Perseus Publishing, 2002).

5. See Erick Schonfeld, "eBay's Secret Ingredient," *Business 2.0*, March 2002.

6. See Jeffrey Rayport, "The Virus of Marketing" *Fast Company*, Issue 6, December 1996, and Steve Jurvetson and Tim Draper, "Viral Marketing" *Business 2.0*, November 1998.

7. "Buzz Marketing: Suddenly This Stealth Strategy Is Hot—But It Is Still Fraught with Risk," *Business Week*, 30 July 2001.

8. Jathon Sapsford, "PayPal Sees Torrid Growth with Money Sending Service," *Wall Street Journal*, 16 February 2000.

9. A good source of background materials on Palm is the Palm Inc. background articles collected in *Business 2.0*'s Web Guide, <http://www.business2.com/webguide/0,1660,71664,00.html> (accessed 29 October 2002).

10. See Melinda Patterson Grenier, "Adobe's Warnock Will Stay in Touch After Retiring," *Wall Street Journal*, 23 March 2001, <http://interactive.wsj.com/public/current/articles/SB985275823472 429409.htm?> (accessed 29 October 2002).

11. Everett Rogers, *The Diffusion of Innovations* (New York: Free Press, 1995).

12. See Robert Berner, "Why P&G's Smile Is So Bright," *Business Week*, 12 August 2002.

Chapter 6

1. See Ira Sager, "NetPCs Are Having a Hard Time Booting Up," *Business Week*, 22 September 1997.

2. The original concepts were developed by John F. Nash, in "The Bargaining Problem," *Econometrica* 28 (1950). For a survey of the literature that followed, see William L. Thomson, "Cooperative Models of Bargaining," in *Handbook of Game Theory*, ed. Robert Aumann and Sergiu Hart (Amsterdam: North-Holland, 1995).

3. For the practical approaches, see Roger Fisher, William Ury, and Bruce Patton, *Getting to YES: Negotiating Agreement Without Giving In*, 2nd ed. (New York: Penguin Books, 1991). For the theoretical approaches, see Martin J. Osborne and Ariel Rubinstein, *Bargaining and Markets* (New York: Academic Press, 1990).

4. See Kurt Oeler and Corey Grice, "AT&T Wins the Bidding War for MediaOne," CNET News.com, <http://news.com.com/2100-1033-225427.html?legacy=cnet> (accessed 29 October 2002).

5. See Fisher, Ury, and Patton, *Getting to YES*.

6. See Steve Glain, "Chinese Outmaneuvered AT&T in Trans-Pacific Cable Project," *Wall Street Journal*, 23 July 1997.

7. A. Michael Spence won a Nobel Prize on the basis of his work on the role of signals between two parties with access to different information. Michael Spence, "Job Market Signaling," *Quarterly Journal of Economics* 87 (1973).

8. Rob Guth, "Merger Ends Qwest Global Crossing Battle," IDG.net, 19 July 1999, <http://www.idg.net/idgns/1999/07/19/MergerEndsQwestGlobalCrossingBattle.shtml> (accessed 29 October 2002).

9. As a rule, postmerger integration efforts are difficult, and Qwest's marriage with US West had a rocky start, moments after the victory in the auction.

10. See "MCI and WorldCom Close $40B Merger," TechWeb News, <http://www.techweb.com/wire/news/1997/10/1097mci.html> (accessed 29 October 2002).

11. Quoted in "The Battle for MCI: The Consumers," *New York Times*, 11 November 1997.

12. David Henry, "Mergers: Why Most Big Deals Don't Pay Off," *Business Week*, 14 October 2002.

Chapter 7

1. See Robert Pool, *Beyond Engineering: How Society Shapes Technology* (Oxford: Oxford University Press, 1997).

2. Steve Jobs, quoted in the series *Triumph of the Nerds*, Public Broadcasting System series, transcript available at <http://www.pbs.org/nerds/part3.html> (accessed 29 October 2002).

3. There have been, however, many thoughtful discussions on each approach. For a discussion on firm commitment and flexibility, see Pankaj Ghemawat, *Commitment: The Dynamic of Strategy* (New York: Free Press, 1991); for a discussion of modularity and constant reshaping of choices, see Shona Brown and Kathleen Eisenhardt, *Competing on the Edge* (Boston: Harvard Business School Press, 1998).

4. See Mike Akkermans, "A Guide to Action for B2B Electronic Payments," 7 December 2001, <http://www.bbv.be/downloads/A%20GuidetoAction.pdf> (accessed 29 October 2002); "E-commerce Opportunities Grow with the Technology," SatyamPlastics.com articles Web page, <http://www.satyamplastics.com/webtop/articles/37/> (accessed 29 October 2002).

5. <http://www.covisint.com/about> (accessed October 29, 2002).

6. See Bhaskar Chakravorti, "Why Microsoft Should Be Left Alone," *New York Times*, 28 May 1998.

7. "Sony's History: Through the Eyes of the Company's Leaders," Sony Information Page, <http://64.35.93.160/companynews/sonybrand/> (accessed 29 October 2002).

8. See Irene Kunii, Cliff Edwards, and Jay Greene, "Can Sony Regain the Magic?" *Business Week*, 11 March 2002.

9. See Claudia H. Deutsch, "At Xerox, the Chief Is Earning (Grudging) Respect," *New York Times*, 2 June 2002.

Chapter 8

1. Stephen Jay Gould, *The Structure of Evolutionary Theory* (Cambridge, MA: Harvard University Press/Belknap Press, 2002).

2. Paul Duguid, "Material Matters: Aspects of the Past and Futurology of the Book," <http://www2.parc.com/ops/members/brown/papers/mm.html> (accessed 29 October 2002).

3. Clayton M. Christensen, *The Innovator's Dilemma: When New Technologies Cause Great Firms to Fail* (Boston: Harvard Business School Press, 1997).

4. Paul David, "Clio and the Economics of QWERTY," *American Economic Review* 75 (1985): 332–337; W. Brian Arthur, *Increasing Returns and Path Dependence in the Economy* (Ann Arbor: University of Michigan Press, 1994). For alternative perspectives on the issue, see Bhaskar Chakravorti, "Why Microsoft Should Be Left Alone," *New York Times*, 28 May 1998; Lee Gomes, "Economists Decide To Challenge Facts of QWERTY Story," *Wall Street Journal*, 25 February 1998; Paul Krugman, "Soft Microeconomics: The Squishy Case Against You-Know-Who," *Slate*, <http://web.mit.edu/krugman/www/soft.html> (accessed 18 December 2002).

5. See Brad Wieners, "Eight Technologies That Will Change the World," *Business 2.0*, June 2002.

6. Benjamin Elkin, *The Loudest Noise in the World* (New York: Junior Literacy Guild and Viking Press, 1954).

INDEX

About the Author

BHASKAR CHAKRAVORTI is Partner and Thought Leader at Monitor Group, the global strategy firm headquartered in Cambridge, MA. He leads Monitor's practice advising the world's preeminent companies on growth strategies that involve high uncertainty and high payoff, through the practical applications of game theory. This work involves some of the most challenging issues that confront CEOs: taking innovations and new technologies to market, managing competitive dynamics, new market entry, M&A, corporate strategy, and shaping industry evolution. He has managed major client relationships with multiple industry leaders and has pioneered Monitor's intellectual property in this area. His focus has been on innovative and evolving industries with complex markets: from telecommunications and high-tech to pharmaceuticals, medical devices, and consumer products.

Prior to Monitor Dr. Chakravorti was in high-tech R&D as a game theorist at Bellcore, formerly the research labs for the Bell telephone companies, and in academia as an economics professor at the University of Illinois at Urbana-Champaign. Before moving to the United States, he was with the Tata Administrative Service, the management arm of India's largest business house.

Dr. Chakravorti has published extensively in academic and policy books; in journals such as *Journal of Economic Theory*, *Journal of Mathematical Economics*, *International Economic Review*, *Journal of Economics and Management Strategy*, *International Journal of Game Theory*, *IEEE Transactions on Automatic Control*; and in the media, including op-eds in the *New York Times*, *Financial Times*, and the *Wall Street Journal Europe*. He has been interviewed on issues relating to technology and globalization in *BusinessWeek* and *Fortune*. He has spoken to audiences in *Fortune* 100 companies; universities; multilateral agencies, including the World Bank; and public-sector agencies on four continents.

He lives in Brookline, Massachusetts, with his wife, two children and, unwillingly, their three cats.

Monitor Group, the global strategy firm, integrates strategy consulting, merchant banking, deal structuring, research, and management education to serve clients through offices in twenty-two countries around the world.